OFF-GRID LIVING

A Step-by-Step, Back to Basics Guide to Become Completely Self-Sufficient In as Little as 30 Days

Small Footprint Press

CONTENTS

INTRODUCTION

Over the past few years, there has been a sudden and powerful interest in leaving the city and finding an independent life in the country. You have probably experienced some of the same thoughts and feelings. There's been a massive departure from some of the densest population centers in the United States. There have been net population losses in New York, Nairobi, and Paris.

People are sick of the noise, the pollution, and the chaos that exists in cities. They want to live in places that feature natural beauty.

In Russia, people are leaving for country estates called *dachas*. In the UK, people are leaving London and Edinburgh for the Scottish highlands. In the USA, people are abandoning San Francisco and New York. We are seeing a great migration from cities worldwide. After the COVID pandemic started in 2019, people didn't want to feel confined anymore. They want to be able to walk outside freely. They don't want to feel dependent on strangers. They don't want to live every day feeling like they need permission for everything.

Unsurprisingly, many people have recently been attracted to living off-grid as it offers relief for many who have been suffocating from these feelings and are ready to get out.

Cities are strange environments that we've created for ourselves. We could have made any kind of place to live, and for some reason, we chose to stack ourselves into tiny little 40-story apartments. We decided that this was worth paying $1,800 in rent every month.

New York had the good sense to set some land aside to feature nature - Central Park. City planners had the foresight to know that if people become too separated from nature, it would crush their spirits and make them feel crazy.

Now we are at a time where we don't even remember why we wanted to live like that. Lots of people are seeing it for the first time.

But off-grid living, unfortunately, is not for everyone. While living off-grid is a wonderful lifestyle, it's a huge step to take, especially for those who don't have any experience living self-sufficiently. It takes time, effort, and money to make these changes, such as buying land far outside the city, setting up off-grid systems, and raising livestock. Furthermore, many people are held back by their assumptions about living off-grid.

There's so much to learn about this lifestyle. Throughout this book, you'll discover that some expectations are far from reality and that the things that you think are holding you back or preventing you from being able to live off-grid don't exist at all. You will learn precisely what off-grid living entails and what you need to do. Once you have all of the information needed, you will be able to make an informed decision about whether off-grid living is for you or not.

Something Better

Think of this book as a shopping catalog. You're building a new life, and you need to figure out all the pieces and how you will put it all together.

This book will cover many topics, but it can't teach you everything you need to know. This one book can't train you to be a plumber, electrician, outdoorsman, carpenter, and farmer. What this book can and will give you is a broad understanding of living off-grid by providing you with information and options to help you decide what's best for you and your family.

Some people enjoy living a simple, minimalistic life free of modern conveniences. Other people can have a completely normal modern lifestyle off the grid. If you want to have a super minimalist, 18th-century lifestyle, that's fine. If you want a modern lifestyle off-grid, that's okay, too. It's just a matter of what you are looking for.

One topic that many people might be interested in that we won't get into is prices. Prices are constantly changing. Wind power and solar technology are improving and becoming more popular, so the prices are decreasing as it becomes more popular in the consumer market. Battery technology is getting better. There are also changes in the price of inflation and some recent political considerations that will affect the availability of imports.

For that reason, this book will not mention the cost. By the time you read this, it may be completely different. You will want to do your own shopping and figure out those costs on your own. While some things are cheaper, and there's no reason to pay more for them, you get exactly what you pay for. Suggesting you get the most expensive Gucci may not be appropriate, and also saying you should get the cheapest one available might be a terrible idea.

CHAPTER 1: IS OFF-GRID LIVING THE RIGHT CHOICE FOR YOU?

Chapter one provides an in-depth overview of what it truly means to live off-grid, what it takes to get there, and whether it's the right path for you to take.

More and more people worldwide are beginning to realize that a life away from modern society's ever-present chaos sounds more plausible and amazing than ever. Because of recent events and the instability of modern life in general, many want to escape to their own slice of heaven, away from civilization and the traps of society.

While people in the city depend on its various systems to survive, they still need to take care of their necessities. The city lacks a sense of community where people are able to depend on each other for their daily lifestyles. Much like a lone wolf, people in the city take care of only themselves and no one else. However, they are also dependent on government structures and institutions to maintain their lifestyles.

On the opposite end, there are self-sustaining communities, where individuals function as a collective by helping each other with their various skills. Their differing skills allow them to live sustainably and sufficiently without needing sources outside of their community!

While they depend on each other to survive, they are very different from people in the city who depend on institutions and government structures. Self-sustaining communities depend on each other to have more freedom, while people in the city depend on their systems, only to be restricted by the very systems they rely on.

They live off-grid, sustaining themselves by growing their own food, raising livestock, harvesting water, and so much more. Each person in the community serves a purpose, so they build each other up, allowing their sustainable way of living to be possible.

While you don't have to be a part of a similar community to live off-grid, they can be viewed as role models because having the mindset that you need to be alone to survive can be disadvantageous in many ways.

What Is Off-Grid Living?

Some people have very rigid ideas of what off-grid really entails, but in reality, off-grid living simply describes a particular lifestyle. Living off-grid is all about self-reliance and self-determination. You have to be aware of nature and what it provides.

Living off-grid isn't always easy, and it isn't for everyone, especially when just starting out. There are many things to learn and trials that will challenge you along the way. Living on your own, developing your self-reliance, and learning to take control of your own needs is not the easiest way to live a life, but it is rewarding. It's one thing to work a job that pays you well and gives you enough for a down payment on a home to live in and raise a family. There's another experience entirely of living in a home that you built.

Living off-grid usually implies being disconnected from the electrical grid, gas, municipal water supply, sewage, and telephone lines. It doesn't mean living without the things that those services provide. It means providing them for yourself.

Living off-grid does NOT mean:

- Living in a medieval hut.
- Abstaining from modern conveniences.
- Cutting off contact from the outside world.
- Growing a beard and living in a bunker while writing a weird manifesto.

There are many reasons why a person would choose to live off the grid. It is a lifestyle that attracts all kinds of people from all kinds of backgrounds. Ask yourself if any of these apply to you.

Green

Disconnecting from the grid means disconnecting from the energy system. Being able to produce your own energy from the sun, wind, or water is a way to reduce your environmental impact. Perhaps you just want to separate yourself from the pollution in the city.

Many people living off-grid have objections to factory farming practices and would rather grow their own food than participate in the industrial food system. You may feel better knowing exactly where your food came from. You can grow what you like and know it is free of GMOs and pesticides.

You may be well aware of the electricity you use at home. But there's also the electricity you don't see on your monthly power bill. That electricity is factored into the price of every manufactured thing you own. Some of those items are manufactured abroad in places with few environmental laws. Many of the things you own may have been built or manufactured using coal or oil energy, which are well-known pollutants. If you reduce your consumption by using the land, you can also reduce your dependence on things you disagree with.

A self-sufficient lifestyle might help you be more conscientious about your own footprint and impact on global climate change. Many people have gotten into off-grid living as part of a movement to take responsibility for their own environmental impacts. You may not be able to change the world, but you can change yourself. If enough people do that, we're all better off.

Self-Reliance

A lot of people simply like to be self-reliant. In the event of a natural disaster, self-sufficiency will not be a problem for a person living off-grid. If the power goes out, they have power. If the water becomes a problem, they have water. If the cost of food spikes or there are shortages, that will not be a problem for a family who grows their own food.

Overall, people just feel a sense of pride and accomplishment. Some people don't want to feel like they are a burden on others and that no one else burdens them. You gain a certain sense of security when you know that you don't need to rely on others. If you only need to rely on yourself and you are reliable, then you'll never be disappointed.

If you want to strike it out, make it on your own, and build something that you can be proud of, homesteading might be the thing for you.

PRIVACY

We all like our privacy: We like quiet and solitude. If you are inclined to walk around your house in the nude, you can do so without worrying about any neighbors peeking into the windows. In fact, you could probably just walk outside completely nude without any fear of phone calls to the police.

If you want to have guests over, play music, and have a bonfire and a good time outside, no one will live close enough to you to complain about it. No one is going to come and knock on your door and tell you to keep down the noise.

Likewise, you don't have to deal with anybody else's noise. When you live in the city, you become accustomed to a lot of ambient noise. You have to hear traffic and cars honking their horns. The occasional car alarm goes off for no apparent reason at 1:00 a.m.; babies scream so loud that you can hear them through the walls of your apartment; and dogs bark, bravely protecting a homeowner from the dangerous pizza delivery guy who just arrived.

Being isolated can also separate you from the problems in the city. If you live in a place with a lot of crime and violence, it tends to stay in that area and not spread too far. Having a place relatively isolated is less likely to be targeted, so long as you take the right precautions.

Investment

You don't have to be a hippie or a bearded mountain man to live off-grid. Sometimes, it just makes sense financially. A large off-grid project can have a significant upfront cost, but over time, it can easily pay for itself from the savings on electric, water, gas, and food bills. Living off-grid may simply make sense for people trying to be thrifty.

If you buy or build a home in a very remote location, it may be way too expensive to get utilities out to your location. For practical reasons, connecting to the grid might just be unrealistic for you—this is more common than you think. Those who have their homes built very high in the mountains or deep in the woods or countryside, without many neighbors, might decide that off-grid living is considerably less expensive than paying to have pipes and electrical lines built all the way to the grid to hook it up.

People who invest in homes often build off-grid homes to rent out to vacationers. Most people don't want to live in a remote place, but many people would love to vacation in a place like that. Turning a remote and rustic off-grid location into a rental or vacation destination through one of the online hotel alternative websites could be a very remunerative enterprise.

Developing an off-grid home can require a good chunk of change. However, all of that money is an investment. Every addition you develop adds to the value of the land and will come back to you when you sell—provided there is no terrible disaster, knock on wood.

There's been an increased interest in leaving the cities in the last few years, and people are escaping into rural areas. One can probably expect the land's value to increase rather than decrease over time. For that reason, having a self-sufficient and isolated spot that appeals to people trying to escape city life could be a valuable property to flip.

How Do I Know if Off-Grid Living Is for Me?

Frankly, it might not be. Off-grid living is not for everybody. It takes a certain kind of personality to take on such a project and commit to it. It takes a lot of self-reliance and eagerness to learn.

People have become very accustomed to convenience. Convenience is another word for time—as in saving time. Anything convenient saves time, but there is also a cost. Fast food is convenient. Ordering cheap things online is convenient. Sometimes, there are things more valuable than convenience. Also, the time that we are trying to save is just being wasted on other frivolous things.

These are some qualities that might determine if you are the kind of person who can do it. You don't need all of them; one is enough, but the more, the better.

Self-Starter

If you like projects, this is a great way to live. You will never run out of things to do. Many people make their home their primary hobby. Are you the kind of person who thinks about a good way to fix a squeaky garage door? Or the kind of person who builds a shed? If you're the kind of person who loves keeping busy and working with their hands, you are in luck.

There are always new ideas you have for additions and upgrades. Once your home is all put together, you'll start imagining other things you could build, such as a sauna or a guest house. Once you are done with those, you may consider what it would take to build an artificial pond. If this sounds like you, keep reading.

Autodidact

That's not a type of dinosaur: An autodidact is a person who teaches themselves rather than being taught by others. You will need to learn a lot to live off-grid. If you don't like learning, this lifestyle will not work for you, as learning will always be important.

Starting this life will make you a jack of all trades very quickly. To achieve absolute self-sufficiency, you will have to learn plumbing, electrical, farming, animal care, local law, and many other skills. Some people see that and want nothing to do with that. Others see a list like that and get excited.

If you like learning and are an inquisitive person who enjoys figuring things out and discovering new things, you will have plenty of opportunities. You will discover all the things you didn't know that you needed to know, and there are a lot.

Able to Follow Through on Commitments

You were meant to be someone who isn't a quitter. Depending on how you develop your land, there can be a significant initial investment. It's possible to get started with $10,000, but depending on various factors, it could cost more. If you aren't serious about it, you could easily waste a lot of time and money.

Pioneers and homesteaders of previous centuries did it with a lot less than we have available. Lucky for you, more tools and technologies are available to you than they had.

By definition, you won't have an infrastructure around you that has been built up over a century by thousands of governments and financial corporations. You have to develop your own infrastructure from the bottom up. Over the long term, it can pay for itself.

This isn't like a month-long free trial at a gym or using a subscription service for a phone app. It's not the kind of thing you can half do half-heartedly. If you are a person who likes to finish what they start and someone who doesn't rush into things, you have the right personality to live off-grid.

A Love for Nature

Last but not least, if you are looking to live off-grid somewhere that is far away from other people, you should be a person who genuinely loves nature. You are going to be surrounded by a lot of it.

Living off-grid means living in tandem with nature. You have to cooperate with it. Mother Nature decides when it rains, when the sun shines, and when the wind blows. While not everyone feels comfortable feeling at the mercy of nature, other people don't feel like they are at nature's mercy, but rather that they are adapting to what nature prescribes. It's a very different attitude.

Maybe you like living in a city where it's easy to find the things you need within a five-minute drive, and you don't like the unpredictability of nature. If you like gardening and animals, you'll have plenty of time with them. If you are someone who loves hiking, skiing, fishing, hunting, and exploring, then this is where you want to be. Are you someone who loves campfires and loves to have their morning coffee on a porch overlooking a beautiful landscape? If so, you have come to the right place.

Healthy and Fit

People with medical issues requiring regular treatments and need to be close to the hospital or visit a clinic regularly are at greater risk if they live far away. Being off-grid doesn't mean you can't be close to a hospital, but if you need a hospital to be close, be sure to factor that in. If you plan on doing the work yourself, you should be healthy and able. People who use wheelchairs might have a very rough time with it. However, if you're in a wheelchair and can build your dream home, that would be very impressive and inspiring.

If you aren't strong or have good cardio, that problem will solve itself. You'll be chopping and carrying wood, building fences, and other physical activities, plus a cellar without junk food—that will get you in a fitter state in no time.

Start Small

Living off the grid also doesn't have to be 100% complete on day one. Sometimes, the smartest way to start is to start small. Once you have a good piece of land with all the features you need, you can get a trailer for relatively cheap to park there. That's a good place to start.

You can buy any water you need and bring it to your location. If you're ready now, go and do it. Take it one step at a time. For most water systems, you'll need a pump. That means you'll need power. Power comes first.

You can start with a gas-powered generator until you can create something more permanent. It won't be long before you've set up a sustainable power system, such as using solar power. Once that's up, you won't need a generator; then, you'll be off the electrical grid.

When you get a good or more-developed method of getting clean water, you can stop buying it. You may have to put out some rain barrels to start with, and that's fine. That'll help supplement any water that you are purchasing. Then, you'll be off the water grid.

You can rely on the grocery store when you begin and slowly phase that out as you build your garden and greenhouse and a coop to raise some chickens. Then you'll be self-sufficient in terms of food.

There's no reason to start with the expectation that you will be completely self-sufficient on day one. Frankly, that's very unrealistic unless you can afford to have people come and completely design your project from the ground up before you even move in. Start small and build out. Develop what you need to as you go.

As we say later on in this book multiple times, there is so much to learn. The best way to learn new things is to do them, so don't overwhelm yourself with many projects. Find one goal that you can accomplish, and work on that. When it's done, continue to the next thing. If you come across any problems along the way, you'll figure them out and learn how to fix them. By the time you've moved to your next project, you'll already be an expert in whatever you just resolved.

You can live off-grid within 30 days, but you cannot build a gigantic off-grid compound with every luxury in 30 days. We don't know if it's possible to lay the foundation, build a house, and install plumbing and wiring in 30 days. In some places, we don't think it's even possible to get a permit for construction within 30 days.

However, you can begin the moment that you have land. If you start small, you can be out there next month building toward something, so if you want to do it, do it sincerely.

MINDSET AND ATTITUDE

The off-grid mentality requires a balanced view of optimism and pessimism. You will need optimism to do the work and to believe in yourself that it can be done. It also needs pessimism because you will need to understand that things will go wrong—things that you cannot predict and things that you should be able to anticipate. Your mantra should match that of the Scouts of America: Always be prepared. Just because your electricity is working doesn't mean that something won't happen to stop the electricity. Just because you have a car and can leave doesn't mean that car will always work. Something happens to the car, and an emergency requires you to get yourself or someone else you live with to a hospital. What is plan B? If plan B fails, what is plan C?

Attitude and mindset are intangible things that you need to equip yourself with. You can't anticipate everything, so you will have to figure it out as you go along. You read this book and probably visited websites, read articles, and watched videos on the Internet, but there will always be things you don't know, like the weight of 14 ounces of mercury. There are also the things you haven't realized you don't know. You can only learn these things when experience places them in front of you, and without any preparation, you will have to adapt and be creative.

One thing to keep in mind is what it means to live isolated or far away from other people. If you are from an urban or suburban area, you take a lot of things for granted. You have to understand what it means to be self-reliant in the context of living far away from people.

Remember that if something goes wrong on your property, you are the first line of defense. If something breaks down, you are the closest person to be able to fix it. You're not going to be able to rely on a landlord to come and have a look at it later the same day. If you need professional help, you'll have to call them up, and they'll have to drive out to you.

Maximize your time and get plenty of supplies when you go to town. You will want to have big trips if you're far from town. That means you should choose a day for any shopping you want to do and get everything done all at once—buying bulk and getting lots of stuff. That means also thinking well in advance about what you will need, not just what you want for dinner tonight. You can't just go downstairs to the Bodega and pick up a sandwich.

If you were injured, you might be far from a hospital. For this reason, we strongly recommend that everyone get some kind of first aid training, especially if you live far away from the nearest emergency room. Living alone, far away from other people, can be risky. If you are not healthy or if you're not doing well, then you probably should have other people with you just in case. Something like a heart attack is much less lethal if you can expect an ambulance to arrive within seven minutes. However, if the nearest ambulance is 29 minutes away, you might be in for a lot of trouble.

This also means self-defense. When you live in an isolated area, the chances that someone will come and mug you, break into your house, or rob you are lower. However, if someone does try to come to your house with intentions, the police may be very far away. For that reason, you will be your own first and last line of defense. That could be surveillance cameras or security lights that detect motion. That could mean being armed. The point is, if it's just you out there, it may mean that nobody's coming to help.

Not having stores and other people available to help you quickly means you need to do what survivalists do. Any person who's into wilderness survival will tell you that you need multiple redundancies. That means if one of your pieces of equipment fails, you need to have a backup. When you are building your system, you will want to integrate multiple redundancies throughout it. That means multiple overlapping systems. If you can get electricity from two or more sources—if one of those sources goes down—you'll always have another as a backup. If you can get water from more than one source, if you have a problem like a pump failing, then it won't be nearly as bad. This is especially true if you are relying on a car. Suppose something goes wrong with your vehicle, and you need to leave the property in a hurry. In that case, you aren't going to have a ride-sharing driver just down the block, so you want to make sure that whatever vehicle you use is in tip-top condition; don't leave anything to chance.

You have to think ahead more than you would in a city. You have to plan further into the future about living without your food and about possible problems with your water and power. You have to think about your health and safety. When aid is always close, you don't have to think about these things. When there's always a grocery store a couple of miles away, you don't think about storing your food to last through the winter. A huge part of living an off-grid mindset is not preparing for the worst—not because it's likely but because something bad will happen eventually. Like the various Scouts of America say, always be prepared.

Kids

Going off-grid as a single person or spouse has certain natural advantages. You only need to care for the needs of two people. Going alone is dangerous because if something were to happen to you, no one would come looking for you. If you live with a spouse, someone will wonder why you didn't go back home.

Having children living off-grid with you has a lot of advantages and difficulties tied up with it. Children have the power to contribute more and more as they grow older, but when they're very young, they consume more than they produce. A six-year-old can help out in small ways, but they need more help than they can give. Around the time a child is ten, their contributions to the family and the amount they eat should be about breakeven. So, for the first decade of human life, they need more than they give. This means that adults need to produce more than they need to cover the difference.

Plus, what is crucial in raising kids is education. Depending on how off-grid you live, you might not have realistic access to schools. You might have ideological disagreements with how the schools are run because of religious or political differences. Maybe you think that you can educate your children better than a state employee. In that case, you will have to homeschool your kids. Perhaps you are perfectly content with the education system, and you have an easy way for your children to go to school and come back. That's perfectly fine. You know what is best for your family better than anyone else.

KEY CHAPTER TAKEAWAYS

- **Lesson #1: What Living Off-Grid Truly Means**

Living off-grid doesn't have to mean being disconnected from everyone and everything. You can still live a comfortable, connected life as long as you practice self-sufficiency and sustainability. Remember, you can make this lifestyle work for the kind of life you dream of.

- **Lesson #2: Off-Grid Living Can be For You**

Living off-grid requires you to have many responsibilities, so you need to be someone who likes to stay busy with tasks each day, takes the initiative to learn, loves nature, strives to be healthy and fit, and is committed to making things work. Decide whether this kind of lifestyle is the right choice for you.

- **Lesson #3: Start Small For Your Journey**

Take on your journey step-by-step, no matter how small. Plan an ideal situation for yourself and be patient as you take on new projects little by little. Not everything has to be perfect already. Things take time; your projects don't have to and shouldn't be the end-all immediately. Build slowly and carefully, and do things at your own pace.

- **Lesson #4: The Off-Grid Mindset**

To have an off-grid mentality, you need a perfect balance of confidence and pessimism. You must always be confident in your abilities to make things work and anticipate any unfortunate situation. You must be completely prepared for anything, so anticipate possible setbacks, emergencies, and disasters and make the necessary arrangements to prepare for them.

So, What Does This All Mean For You?

It's your choice to take charge of your life and make the changes. There are many things to consider, but ultimately, the decision lies in the kind of person you are, your determination, and your desires for your and your family's lives.

You probably realize that a self-sufficient life is more challenging to achieve. You'll learn in-depth information throughout this book, but if you want more hands-on learning and insider resources, you'll want to book a call with us today.

Take control of your life and transform everything you know about an off-grid lifestyle. Achieve it faster and easier than you could ever imagine.

Off-Grid Mindset Check-in Exercise

Before we proceed with the rest of the book, let's first explore where you are right now in your Off-Grid Journey.

Below, rate yourself on a scale of one to five on how accurate the statements are for you - a score of one means "not accurate," and a score of five means "very accurate."

After you have rated yourself according to the statements, add the sum total of your scores, then read "What Your Score Really Means" to determine the outcome of your results.

Check-in Statement	**Rating**
I am completely sure that I want to live off-grid.	
I have an idea of what it takes to be self-sufficient.	
I know what my responsibilities will be when I live off-grid.	

I have an idea of a budget for my off-grid living expenses.	
I have a timeline for myself to live off-grid.	
I have begun making plans for my journey.	
I know how and what I will eat once I live off-grid.	
I am aware of the reasons I have for living off-grid.	
I know the basic fundamentals needed to live off-grid.	
My expectations and assumptions about living off-grid are in line with its realities.	
TOTAL SCORE:	

What Your Score Really Means

Score: 0 - 15

The Fundamentals of the Off-Grid Mindset are Still Missing

The news here is that your current knowledge about living off-grid is missing at its core. You might be feeling a bit clueless about things, or you may even have no idea where to start. It can be a steep learning curve for those just starting out, but the good news is you can fix it.

At this stage, knowing more about the fundamentals of living off-grid is the best place to start. Understanding how it works and your responsibilities will give you a better idea of how things will go for you. Studying more about it from the chapter will help you get over the hump and eventually lead you to know where you need to be.

Score: 16 - 30

Reviewing Will Enlighten Your Mindset

Your knowledge on living off-grid is getting there, but there are some things you'll need to tweak. Learning won't be enough if you cannot retain the information you get. So, throughout the chapter, take note of all the responsibilities you'll be taking on when you live off-grid. Make sure to review everything you'll need to plan and prepare, such as choosing a power or water system beforehand.

Score: 31+

You're Ready to Plan to Live Off-Grid

You already have a good understanding of being self-sufficient and your responsibilities once you begin your venture. Now it's time to plan everything. Having knowledge won't help you in your journey if you don't choose to apply it as well. It's time to take action.

When you plan, it's good to set short-term and long-term goals. Ask yourself what the timeline is that you would like to follow to complete certain tasks. You can also begin by listing down everything you need to learn and plan for. From there, writing out your budget and your plan of action will surely help you get things in order.

Chapter 2: Location, Location, Location

Chapter two will focus on how you can look for the perfect land for your future home, the best locations all over the world and in the United States to live off-grid, and the factors to consider when you finally decide on your plot of land.

Imagine this: you finally have your perfect off-grid home. You have a generous plot of arable land, a charming house you call your own, and maybe even some farm animals strutting around.

The sun has risen, and you wake up to a view of rolling hills, a bright blue sky, and soft sunlight coming in through your window. It's so serene that you can't help but smile right as you get out of bed. Your home is so pleasantly warm and cozy despite the cold weather outside. You have power to heat your home and running water to boil for your morning coffee.

You step out to collect fresh eggs from your coop, sweet honey from your bee colony, and creamy goat milk straight from your backyard, just in time for breakfast. You breathe in a gentle breeze drifting by, and it smells so fresh and crisp as if it had just rained.

You spend the rest of your day tending to your garden and animals, reading a lovely book, with nothing else to worry about but taking care of yourself, your home, and your loved ones.

Of course, imagining your future home is far easier than making it happen. When you start to get serious about living off-grid, you'll find many things to learn, one of which is looking for the best land and location for your future home.

This is one of the most challenging and crucial parts of your journey because once you buy that plot of land, there's no return from it besides shelling out hard-earned cash. And none of us wants that.

That's why, before you even decide, you need to set factors in place to keep you going in the right direction. If you have no idea what to consider at first and where to start looking for land, you can quickly become one of those people who buy a place out of excitement but end up realizing it's not close to how they envisioned it to be.

You see, there are several factors to keep in mind when choosing a location. How important each factor is to you will determine your priorities and where you'll purchase land. You can't have your dream off-grid home without thorough research, and since this takes a lot of time, you might reach your goals a bit further down the road than expected.

And that's why in this chapter, you'll get a rundown of everything you'll need to keep in mind when you start choosing your land and location.

You'll also get a complete outline of the best states to live off-grid in the United States and even countries worldwide. These will automatically rule out the wrong places for you and shine a light on the right ones! You won't have to trade in those precious hours anymore for research; instead, start working on your goals.

After reading this, you'll be ready with a checklist and a design concept for your ideal off-grid home. Your own beautiful home tucked away in paradise, with total freedom and basking in nature, are within reach, all at your fingertips as you flip through these pages.

When you plan to live off-grid and look for your own location, you must remember how you should treat that area as your own sacred place. You must learn how to show respect, importance, and care for it, similar to how the Indigenous Americans do.

The historical values of Indigenous Americans hold a deep respect and appreciation for nature. Because of this, they made sure to take care of their surroundings, including the lives of humans, animals, trees, and plants.

As a community, their daily toils centered on maintaining the space around them and building up resources. Wherever they were in America, Indigenous Americans held a pearl of similar wisdom: that when you take care of nature, nature will take care of you. They knew that each part of the Earth was crucial for their overall survival. Each part was dependent on the other to thrive. And for nature to do its part, humans must also step in and care for them.

These values that the Indigenous Americans held so tightly are not as revered now in modern cultures. But now, it's time to look past ourselves and find a more profound outlook on how the world works. We must observe and appreciate how nature plays a huge part in caring for us, so we must do the same for it.

Living off-grid also means living off the land. The place you select will have more impact on your off-grid lifestyle than any other factor.

Living off-grid is dealing with the uncertainty of nature.

Choosing a place is a tremendous commitment. If you are going to put all the work into making a place sustainable, it needs to be the right place. You don't want to put a lot of time, money, and energy into something only to realize that it can't work for you. You need to really plan ahead. If you are close with your family, then being far apart from them might be a deal-breaker.

Location will determine a lot about the way you live. Your access to water, the soil, and other natural features will determine the energy sources and other resources available to you. The laws can be as important, if not more important, in determining how you get your water and electricity, how you heat and cool your home, and even what you eat. Make no mistake: Choosing where you live is going to be the most crucial decision, and there are many factors you need to balance.

How to Find the Perfect Off-Grid Location

What is important to you will ultimately depend on you. No one can better determine what your needs are and what kind of life you prefer. As we said in the introduction, this book is like a catalog of options that you can choose from.

Soil

If you are going to be doing any farming, the quality of the soil is going to be very important. You don't want to put all the energy into starting a farm on land that won't give anything to yield. An easy way to determine if the land is good is just to simply look around. Are other people farming in this area? If they are, there's a good chance they know what they are doing and are using farmland.

This isn't a deal-breaker by any means. If the soil isn't great, you can buy soil at any home improvement store, add your own nitrogen, and use your compost to keep the earth mineral-rich. Using your own earth, you can build a garden using raised garden beds for vegetables and herbs.

Not all locations are appropriate for all kinds of farming. Depending on the season, soil, and climate, certain crops will be more amenable than others. For example, you aren't likely to find many tomato farmers in Alaska.

Climate

When living off-grid, you are dependent on nature to provide for you. That should go without saying, but the climate will be crucial to how you organize your life. Different climates have different advantages and disadvantages that you will need to weigh to make the life you want.

Warmer climates are usually suitable for planting. However, you will have to deal with the problem of cooling yourself and any animals you have. It's much harder to cool down than it is to warm up.

Likewise, wetter climates usually mean more water. They also mean humidity, which isn't great for humans but is excellent for plants. Humidity also usually corresponds with plant growth. Many plants can block out the wind and sun, making generating electricity more difficult if you rely on solar and wind.

A nearby pond might be great for drawing water and raising fish, but it might also be a potential breeding ground for mosquitoes.

Dry environments tend to be more comfortable. Arid areas also usually have more sun and wind, which is great for generating power. However, it may mean that getting water is more difficult or more expensive. Getting water is very important. Humans consume a lot of it, and your plants and animals will, too.

One elementary and important consideration is whether you can even reach your plot of land. Suppose your home is far away from the nearest road and you have lots of snowfall. In that case, you might be at risk of getting snowed in, and unlike other people who live in the city and its subdivisions, there is no truck already on its way to plow the snow for you. Having a long road and heavy snow could mean you'll need a truck that you can mount a snow plow onto.

That's a lot of double-edged swords. There are advantages and drawbacks to everything. You have to seriously consider and weigh what is right for you.

Growing Season

Tied to climate and soil is the growing season. Historically, farmers plant in the spring, grow in the summer, harvest in the fall, and rely on their surplus during the winter. If you are going to be heavily reliant on producing your own food, you will want a longer and more productive season. You probably won't be growing much during the winter.

Building a greenhouse can maximize productivity and extend the season if it is short. The more you grow and effectively store, the deeper you can fill your pantries to enjoy those supplies throughout winter. Luckily if you run out of food, you still have the option of driving to the local grocery store.

Water

The importance of water cannot be understated. When living in arid places like parts of New Mexico and Australia, people are highly dependent on water infrastructure. There is very little rainfall and very little access to natural water supplies.

Without water, you cannot drink, maintain plants or animals, take showers, cook most foods, or even wash your clothes or dishes. You need water, and getting water is your most important and most challenging task.

Your primary water source will come from a well supplemented by rainfall. If you are lucky enough to have rivers or creeks that pass through your property or a pond—provided that there are no regulations against using that water—you can also use those.

The Law

This is the least fun and least interesting part of off-grid living, but it is vital. Making an error about the law can cost you a lot of money and trouble down the road. There's no point in using common sense because laws often don't make sense. Don't assume that you are doing it right without checking first.

The different states have completely different regulations regarding building structures, digging wells, hunting, fishing, and everything else you can imagine. The number of laws is so vast and complex that we even have an entire profession dedicated to arguing about what the laws actually are. They're called lawyers, and even they need to specialize in particular areas of the law because there are so many.

If you aren't sure whether something you were doing is legal or not, we strongly recommend that you don't just guess. You need to investigate for yourself. Reach out to any local boards or administrative offices that handle that sort of thing—that means the DNR or the mayor's office. Even if they can't help you, they may be able to point you toward someone else who can.

Another useful resource is people who are also already living the lifestyle you are working towards. They have most likely already experienced legal hiccups along the way, and if you can reach out to them, they can save you a lot of trouble. Look around on the Internet for forums and groups that are into off-grid living. If you can find others who live in a particular area, they might have answers to your questions.

Never ever buy land in a subdivision. Subdivisions are parcels that are pieces of land, part of a larger covenant agreement. If you have land that is attached to such an agreement, that means you are going to have a lot more rules that you need to follow. It's like having a homeowners' association and a bunch of neighbors who might have very strong opinions about what you can and cannot do with your land. This isn't just true in the suburbs. You can also find properties like this in rural areas, so be sure to avoid this.

Keep in mind that agriculturally zoned land tends to be cheaper than residential or commercial land. If you can, buy agricultural land and make sure it allows for livestock ownership and farming. If you buy land zoned incorrectly, you might find that many things you want to do are not legal.

Believe it or not, some counties legally require you to hook up to city water. Whether you want to or not, you may be forced to pay for installing the pipes and hook up. This can cost you up to $10,000 or more. The same goes for electricity. Some states legally require you to be on the grid. The whole point is to be off-grid, so don't go buying a place where you are not allowed to be off-grid.

There are also considerations of covenants and regulations about whether or not you can have a camper or trailer on your land, or rules about mineral rights or requirements about a permanent foundation. You might find that a big part of choosing your land is whether you can negotiate the obstacles your state and local government set up.

Taxes and Exemptions

Tax laws are quite different from state to state. You may have to pay a rather hefty fee annually, depending on the size and location of the land you are using. Depending on your budget, this cost could be an essential part of your evaluation of where to homestead. Some places have no income tax; some places have low land taxes. These are things to take into account, depending on your finances.

Certain states offer certain tax write-offs that you can avail yourself of. A few states, including Oregon and Utah, offer tax deductions for using green energy on your property. Some states also offer tax breaks for those who use their land for farming. If you are building a new sizable grow operation, you might find that these rebates are worth your while.

Some states offer what's called the homestead exemption. That means that if you happen to go bankrupt and a certain portion of your land is filed as a homestead, then that portion of your land cannot be taken by creditors. The old traditional form of pharmacy went under during bad times, and workers would ultimately lose their homes—this is a law designed to protect people like that. You may not be terribly concerned about going bankrupt, which may not be a factor for you, but it is nice to have everything the same, just in case.

Cost of Living

Money always matters. You may have a lot, or you may have a little. Your budget is your business, and budgeting might be a crucial factor for you.

Typically, the farther you are from the city, the cheaper the land will be. People will pay a pretty penny to be close to a hospital or inside a good school district. The farther away you are from all of that, the less you need to spend. You might have to balance how close you want to be to civilization with how much you're willing to spend.

Banks and mortgage companies like to sell you houses, not dirt. Sometimes, finding banks willing to finance vacant land can be challenging. Often, the banks selling empty land charge more in terms of interest or down payments. One way around this is to work out a deal directly through owner financing. In this case, the bank operates as an intermediary where the lending agreement is directly between the current owner and the prospective buyer. The bank just gets a taste of mediating.

Everyone lives on different budgets; some places are more expensive than others. The prices of things are based on whatever the market will bear. Things you want, such as natural beauty, will also be valuable to other people. This is one reason why locations like Geneva and Southern California are so expensive. Both have great weather. Switzerland has access to a beautiful mountain range and nature, and California has an entire coastline and beaches galore. And of course, living near people with money costs money.

If you were living in a particularly remote area, things would simply be more expensive because of the challenge of supplying areas. Areas in or around Alaska or island systems in places like Canada and Southeast Asia can be quite pricey because shipping to them is costly and complex.

Natural Disasters

God forbid that you should experience any serious natural disaster. The odds that your home will be affected by one like that is usually pretty remote, but it shouldn't be ignored. You need to investigate if the area you're homesteading in is particularly vulnerable to flooding, tornadoes, or hurricanes. You need to think about these things and have a plan ready so that you will know ahead of time and have a way to protect yourself.

Communication is essential for this. If you live in an area prone to getting tornadoes, you definitely need access to the national weather service and a place to take shelter, such as a cellar. You don't want to be the last person to know there's a tornado with no good way of getting away or taking shelter.

HOMESCHOOLING

School is very important for people who have kids or plan on having kids. It matters in terms of quality but also accessibility.

If you live far away from any schools, you might not have a bus that comes by your home. It might not be realistic to drive your kids to school and back, depending on the distance. Or perhaps you want to homeschool for ideological reasons.

Whatever the case may be, homeschooling might be important to you. Not all states are equally permissive about homeschooling. You will want to look into this and ensure that your state will allow it if that's important to you.

If you do decide to take the homeschooling route, now is a better time than ever. Homeschooling has come a long way over the last 20 years. There are all kinds of programs and lessons that can be bought online. There are many ways to meet with other parents and children to help them learn to socialize.

Access to Civilization

Some people can't safely live in an isolated area. If you have an illness requiring frequent doctor visits or hospital visits, it might not be the best idea to live far from access to medical services.

Living off-grid does not mean you are living like a caveman or a 19th-century Canadian lumberjack. Being off a utility grid does not mean being off a social grid. You don't need to be socially isolated from other people. In fact, every psychologist will strongly recommend that you do not isolate yourself from other people. Just because you are living off-grid does not mean that you can't go into town to pick up supplies or go out to dinner or sports events.

The distance you are from your closest ER or grocery store might make a massive difference in driving time, gas, and emergency response. Being located in a spot that is difficult for an ambulance to get to might be a deal-breaker.

Best States for Off-Grid Living

These are ten of the best states for living off-grid. This is not a top ten list; they aren't ranked from worst to best. Each of these places has its own strengths and weaknesses. Which is "best" depends on your needs and wants. No place is perfect for everyone, but there is a place that is perfect for you.

Look over this list and measure the pros and cons; from there, you can decide which place you feel is best.

North Carolina

"Nothing could be finer than to be in Carolina in the morning." North Carolina is a fantastic farm state, and many fellow homesteaders are out there because of their very friendly laws. Plus, since it's a great farming state with a long growing season and beautiful agriculture, it also happens to be expensive. North Carolina is a lovely state, and you get what you pay for.

Pros

- It is a big farm state
- There are a lot of homesteaders, and it is ideal out west
- Green rebate
- Homestead declaration
- It has a long growing season

Cons

- Expensive land
- They are tight on homeschooling

Michigan

The wolverine state is not a bad choice at all. One of its most obvious and valuable features is that there is a ton of fresh water. Enormous lakes surround the state, and tons of smaller lakes are on the interior. No one living in Michigan is too far away from a place to take a boat out to relax or to go fishing.

Michigan already has a substantial homesteading community, and you are better off finding plenty of other like-minded people. The more north you decide to venture into the state, the more open land there is.

One thing Michigan isn't running out of is fresh water. Michigan has all four seasons, although winters may seem a little long. The land is good for raising crops, but the season might be short. Maximize the season.

Michigan is also a great state for fishing. There are more lakes than you can count and plenty of salmon and trout that you can catch.

Michigan also has a large homesteading community. Having people who are also taking on the same project is always great; by making friends with others, you can learn a lot. In recent years, the price of living in Michigan has increased, so consider that.

Pros

- The soil is good
- It has short seasons
- There is a lot of water for fishing
- There are many other homesteaders

Cons

- The laws can be strict
- It has middle-of-road taxes
- It has complicated homeschooling laws

TENNESSEE

The beautiful state of Tennessee is one of the most underrated in the Union. Like North Carolina, Tennessee is a state that is very friendly to homesteaders. It also happens to be the state that hosts The Great Appalachian Homesteading Conference. While Idaho is getting a lot of love right now, the people of Tennessee should be glad that they haven't been discovered quite yet.

People living off-grid are generally more likely than most others to get nailed with a ton of natural disasters. Anyone living out there needs to take the proper precautions.

Pros

- It has a mild climate with four distinct seasons
- It's a beautiful state with great state and national parks
- The cost of living is relatively low—it's about 10% less than the national average
- There's good dirt for farming, especially in the west
- There is plentiful water
- Rural Homesteading Land Grant
- It has a homestead exemption

Cons

- There are lots of natural disasters, including earthquakes, tornadoes, and floods

INDIANA

Like many other places on this list, Indiana is great for farming. They've got a good assortment of land and a good growing season; they aren't hurting for water. At present, picking up rural land in Indiana may be tricky, so be sure to keep an eye out well in advance if you have any desire to move out there. One last thing, and we say this with all due respect, Indiana, besides homesteading, is a pretty dull state. If you like boring, that's great. If that's going to be a problem for you, maybe look around for other items on this list.

Pros

- It mostly features farmland
- It has a longer growing season
- It has good homeschooling systems
- The income tax is good

Cons

- It might not be easy to get land
- It has high sales taxes

IOWA

Iowa is, of course, an excellent farming state. They offer generous tax credits for farmers and homestead exemption, which is definitely a big help.

With no disrespect to the good people of Iowa, Iowa is not a very pretty state. It is mostly rolling planes filled with corn, wheat, and soybeans. It doesn't enjoy the beautiful forests of Northern California or the mountains of Tennessee and Colorado. It doesn't have beautiful bodies of water like Michigan or Florida. Iowa has many good qualities, but the natural aesthetic is not one of them.

Pros

- It is a big farming state
- It offers tax credits for farming
- There are homestead exemptions
- It has low taxes
- Homeschooling is allowed

Cons

- There are a lot of floods
- Let's be honest. Iowa isn't beautiful. Sorry, Iowa.

VIRGINIA

Virginia is a fantastic farming state and always has been. They have a lot of rainfall, and they have access to the ocean. It's a trendy state for a good many reasons.

However, the problem with popular states is that they attract many people. Many people mean more expensive land, a higher cost of living, and higher taxes. There are many disadvantages of living in a city, and in Virginia, those disadvantages will follow you into the more isolated areas.

Pros

- There's great farming—Virginia is a farming state and always has been.
- It has good rainfall
- It has low property tax
- You can sell back electricity to power
- It is very popular

Cons

- The land is expensive
- The cost of living is high
- They are strict on homeschooling
- The state is quite disaster-prone: hurricanes and flooding

OREGON

Once you leave the Portland area, you will feel like you're in a completely different country. Oregon is a geologically beautiful state and very wet. Finding water in Oregon is as difficult as throwing a rock and waiting to hear it splash on something. You'll pay a hefty income tax if you make a lot of money, though.

Pros

- There are no sales taxes
- There's lots of water
- There are few natural disasters
- It has a green energy tax rebate
- It's very rainy

Cons

- It has a high income tax

MISSOURI

Missouri is very friendly to homesteads. They are very light with regulations, which is a significant hurdle to overcome in more regulated states. The state is also geologically diverse, and one part of the state will be quite different from another one. In short, it's easier to do what you want with your property.

Missouri gets a lot of rain. An average of about 40 inches per year, and it is legal to collect rainwater in barrels ("Average Annual Precipitation for Missouri," n.d.). Summers are sweltering and can get very humid, but the winters are a little milder. By that, we mean a longer growing season but more need to keep your home cool.

Pros

- It has long seasons
- It has a good amount of rainfall
- It's a great place for homeschooling
- There are solar incentives

Cons

- The winters are rough
- It has high income taxes
- There are natural disasters like tornadoes and floods

Wyoming

The cowboy state is a strong option. It is the least populated state in the Union, and the land is cheap. There is plenty of open space for solar and wind. However, sometimes too much of a good thing is a bad thing. Wyoming can have very powerful windstorms that are so strong that the roads are shut down for the safety of drivers. If you are in a location that is vulnerable to wind, you could find yourself in some trouble. Also, windmills might be great in most conditions, but powerful winds can sometimes be too much for them to handle.

Wyoming also happens to be a pretty dry state. It is also relatively vulnerable to fires between the dryness and the strong winds. Wildfires are a fact of life in Wyoming.

Pros

- It features tons of open land
- Plots of land are low cost

- It's great for farming
- The cost of living is low
- There's no income tax
- They are relaxed about homeschooling
- It's suitable for solar power
- It's windy

Cons

- There's not much rain, and many wildfires

Idaho

Idaho might be America's best-kept secret. People already living there and know this don't want anyone else to know it, too. They like it the way it is and don't want to see it getting filled up with city people who are fleeing places like Los Angeles and Portland coming in and ruining it. They will usually treat you well if you don't tell anyone that you are from California.

Pros

- Great farmland and resources to help with farming
- The cost of living is low here
- It offers green energy benefits
- It has many homeschool-friendly options

Cons

- The taxes are high
- There are many natural disasters

A Few Great Spots Outside of the US

The US is great for homesteading and off-grid living, but it is far from the only country you can go to. There are very innovative and adventurous homesteading communities all over the world. Here are a few of our favorites.

Raoul Island, New Zealand

As anyone who has watched *The Lord of the Rings* movies knows, New Zealand is one of the most beautiful countries on Earth. The climate is fantastic, and you can live in paradise. Raoul Island is a small island with a small population. Almost everyone there lives completely or partially off-grid.

Pros

- The off-grid community is already there
- It has an excellent climate
- It features unbelievable scenery
- It has great fishing spots

Cons

- Outside supplies need to be shipped in
- It is not cheap

Lasqueti Island, Canada

Located in Vancouver, British Columbia, Lasqueti Island is home to about 400 people living in an off-grid community. If you've never been, Vancouver Island is gorgeous and has everything you need. Vancouver Island has several privately owned islands, so if you are looking to relocate to an excellent off-grid location, you should probably check them out. They are happy to see any visitors who want to check the place out.

Pros

- It features a beautiful environment
- There's great access to fresh water
- There's access to fish
- There's a community of professionals who can help you

Cons

- It can be challenging to get a work permit in Canada
- It's an island, and the only way to leave is by boat or ferry

Khula Dharma, South Africa

Khula Dhamma is an "eco-village," an experiment in green living. People live in updated versions of traditional African huts made with straw and clay, which provide excellent insulation against Africa's hot climate. This community is self-reliant. They produce their own food, electricity, and water.

Pros

- Anyone looking to be green will love this place
- Very knowledgeable bunch of people
- It is inexpensive

Cons

- It may be too rustic for some people
- There is an application process to join the community

- It is very hot

Off-Grid Homes

Living in a home you built creates a certain intimacy with your environment that's difficult to put into words. People who have done it understand this even if they've never tried to articulate it.

Imagine you live in a place where every single board is there because you put that board there. Every single nail was hammered into place with your own hands. You know every inch of the electrical systems. All the pipes are exactly where you chose to put them. You know how all of these systems work because you couldn't have put them there without knowing it. Better yet, inside of this house are memories of the trials, difficulties, and problems that came along while you were building the home. Each of those memories is a fond one because it is a memory of a challenge you overcame.

The self-made home contains the story of the conquest over challenges and the pride of doing it yourself. You will live inside a shrine of your own accomplishments. It's not easy to put a price on that.

There are stories of people who are offered large amounts of money to sell their homes to developers who aren't interested in the home itself but are interested in the land for a larger project. You'll often hear these stories of people who are later refusing to sell at any price. They're living in a home they built themselves or built by their parents or their spouse. It's one thing to live in a place for a long time and call it home. It's another thing to create a home.

Fair Warning

Before doing any work on your property, it is vital that you investigate the laws in your state or country to make sure you aren't accidentally breaking any. Every place is different, and there's no reliable way to know what you can and cannot do by just using your own common sense. You may need to purchase permits; you may need to use licensed contractors. We would recommend that you reach out to your local government. Call them, or even better, show up in person and ask them directly.

In one example we know of personally, a person dug their own well on a property. There was nothing illegal about that; however, for someone to get a bank loan to purchase the property, they needed it to be inspected. During that inspection, they noticed that the well was not installed by a person with state certification. The banks would not loan money to anyone to purchase the property without the certification by the well digger. The owner would have to destroy the well and replace it with another one or find someone willing to purchase the property upfront in cash. Needless to say, it was a huge disaster.

A mistake like this can mean you waste your money with whatever development you're putting into it; you'll also have to waste money to tear down whatever development you made on the property and then waste even more money doing it the prescribed way. If you accidentally violate an ordinance, you will be fined over and over until the issue is settled. If you can't settle it, the state could take your land from you to pay off the debts from the fines that you can't pay.

Do not make the mistake of assuming you know what the rules are. Unless you are an expert and have a career developing in that area, you must double-check everything.

Cabin or House

It's the most obvious living situation, and that's why it's the first one. This is going to be the option that most people will go with if they plan on staying on the property long-term. Houses are not easy projects, as any homeowner will tell you. When you add on the additional challenges of off-grid living, that means there will be a few other considerations to be mindful of.

Building a cabin has a lot of rewards, though. If you have a family, you will need a place big enough for all of them. If you are laying down roots and really trying to start a life somewhere, this is a good choice. Building a cabin is a sensible choice if you are simply trying to improve the land so that you can rent out your property to Airbnb, small rentals, or eventually sell it.

If you have a big family and need a house, build a house. If it's just you and you are starting small, don't feel like you need to jump into this right away. If you don't need a house, don't get one until you do.

In some rare cases, you might renovate an older place and retrofit it to work off-grid. This can be harder than just building a new place from scratch. A lot of off-grid resources are most efficient when they are integrated with the house. It's difficult to build something like a radiant heat floor if the floor is already built. Some old houses might be great candidates for renovation, but I'd recommend against it unless you really know what you are doing.

You may want to pay to have a house built or build some of it yourself and hire contractors for other parts. You may not feel qualified to lay a foundation or install an electrical system. If you are a DIY kind of person and you have the time to do the work yourself, it can be a great experience. If you are an experienced contractor, you can just continue to the next chapter because you probably already know exactly what you're going to build.

Yurt

There's always a yurt for the homesteader who wants to live a more old-fashioned and primitive lifestyle. Not everyone wants to keep all the luxuries and indulgences of modern civilization—many people would like to get away from those things. These are small, one-room buildings. Some people will build several on their property, so everyone living there has their own.

These can be very nice and well done. Yurts are very affordable, cozy, and charming. Yurts are not always great if you want a lot of privacy from other people you share the property with. They are also a project that is doable for the layperson. A house is a lot, but a nice yurt is within reach of someone who isn't a pro but would like to make their own home.

Vehicle

Some people like to live in a vehicle. This is a neat option if you don't like staying around in one place for a long time. If you are in a position in life where you like to travel, you can bring a lot of your home with you. Maybe your land is where you call home, but you move around enough that it just makes sense to live in a home with wheels and an engine. You can have a power and water system waiting for you when you come home.

Living in a vehicle doesn't always mean living in a camper. There is a large community that likes to refurbish and retrofit large vehicles to live in them. This could mean something as small as a van, but people have gone as far as refurbishing former ambulances with excellent suspension systems for traversing difficult mountainous areas. Some people have fixed up vehicles that are out of service or retired school buses and rebuilt them into serviceable homes. There's a tremendous amount of interest in creativity in this lifestyle. Do an Internet search for "van life," and you'll see how popular this trend is, especially with young people.

Shipping Container

It's more common than you may realize, but people have built homes and even larger compounds out of shipping containers—those large rectangular boxes made of corrugated steel that they used to ship goods across the ocean.

If you search on the Internet for many of these things, you might be very impressed with what you find. People have designed remarkably modern and interesting homes by stacking containers and welding them together. They look a lot nicer than we are describing them, and obviously, a lot of work is put into achieving that. There's also been a recent surplus of shipping containers after the COVID-19 pandemic, so getting them now is cheaper than ever.

One technique is to bury the container mostly with dirt with one end of it open. This essentially looks like a hill with a door on the side of it, like a hobbit's home you would see in *The Lord of the Rings*. The drawback here is that you will need a heavy machine to move that much dirt, and you will not have any windows because it is essentially underground. On the plus side, it feels kind of cool, and it has fantastic insulation. When you are mostly underground, you essentially use a geothermal conditioning system that keeps your home warmer in winter and colder in the summer.

Micro Home, AKA Tiny House

Micro homes are a strange and adorable trend. These are exactly what they sound like: They are super small, efficiently organized—and very cheap—homes. You can buy a lot of them almost entirely put together.

Think of them as recreational vehicles without wheels and much nicer overall.

People have also taken tiny houses and built tiny house communities. They are small enough to be easily taken to even tiny plots of land. People who live in these are often off-grid and rely on a lot of solar and wind power, as well as rainwater. If you can comfortably fit your life inside a New York apartment, you can live in a tiny house. This is a really great option for someone young and single, but definitely not an option for people with families who need space.

KEY CHAPTER TAKEAWAYS

- **Lesson #1: Your Location Means Everything**

Your chosen location determines your lifestyle. It will shape your access to water, soil, and other resources. It will also determine the laws in that area regarding how you can access water, electricity, heating, cooling, and nutrition. There are many factors to consider that will help you decide where you want to live.

- **Lesson #2: The Perfect Location For You**

Living off-grid requires you to have many responsibilities, so you need to be someone who likes to stay busy with tasks each day, takes the initiative to learn, loves nature, strives to be healthy and fit, and is committed to making things work. Decide whether this kind of lifestyle is the right choice for you.

- **Lesson #3: The Best US States For Living Off-Grid**

Take on your journey step-by-step, no matter how small. Plan an ideal situation for yourself and be patient as you take on new projects little by little. Not everything has to be perfect overnight. Things take time; your projects don't have to and shouldn't be the end-all immediately. Build slowly and carefully, and do things at your own pace.

- **Lesson #4: The Types of Off-Grid Homes**

To have an off-grid mentality, you need a perfect balance of confidence and pessimism. You must be completely prepared for everything, anticipate possible setbacks, emergencies, and disasters, and make the necessary arrangements to prepare for them. You must always be confident in your abilities to make things work and also anticipate any unfortunate situation.

THE NEXT BEST STEP FOR YOU

Reading and learning about all of this at once can be overwhelming, especially for beginners. There can also be growing pressure on yourself when you start to look for your future home. You might be second-guessing despite researching thoroughly. But you don't have to do things on your own. With us, you can do things step-by-step and be sure of your decisions as we guide you along in your journey.

OFF-GRID LOCATION CHECK-IN EXERCISE

Before we proceed with the rest of the book, let's first explore where you are right now in your Off-Grid Journey.

Below, rate yourself on a scale of one to five on how accurate the statements are for you—a score of one means "not accurate," and a score of five means "very accurate."

After you have rated yourself according to the statements, add the sum total of your scores, then read "What Your Score Really Means" to determine the outcome of your results.

Check-in Statement	Rating
I have begun researching locations for my off-grid home.	
I know what kind of off-grid home I want to live in.	
I have chosen the location for my off-grid home.	
I know the kind of climate I prefer for my location.	
I have chosen whether I'll build or buy a house.	
I have a budget plan for my future home.	
I am aware of the laws and regulations of the location I want to live in.	
I have applied the factors in my decisions for my off-grid location.	
I am aware of the tax laws in my chosen location.	

I am aware of the cost of living in my chosen location.	
TOTAL SCORE:	

WHAT YOUR SCORE REALLY MEANS

Score: 0 - 15

Lack of Information is Holding You Back

Choosing your location for your future home is one of the most challenging parts when starting this venture. It can be a lot of pressure knowing that it will be your home for years to come. Not to mention, it's not cheap, especially when there's already a house built.

You need to ensure you've got everything in order before purchasing your own home. Not being sure about your choices mostly happens when you don't have enough information on the subject, so gathering enough can help you make the correct decisions. Knowing all of your options will make the decision-making process smoother.

Score: 16 - 30

Start Setting Milestones

You've researched enough and know the ropes, but you still don't feel ready to officially buy the lot. Or perhaps you're second-guessing the design of your home. When this happens, setting milestones for yourself as you plan is best.

Create a milestone for completing your research process, choosing a location, or even building your house. This can help you look to the future and know what's in store for you.

Score: 31+

Time to Start Searching for Your Future Home

You have mastered the researching phase, and you're well aware of where you want to be. Now it's time to take a step further and actually buy the lot. There may be a few issues that will come up, such as the timing not being quite right yet, the need to save up more money, or certain conflicts with work or other people.

It's at this moment that you should reevaluate everything. Take note of your ideal situation and compare it to what's possible at the moment. As you go on, your expectations can change to be in line with what can work, and you'll finally reach your goals.

Chapter 3: Off-Grid Water System

In Chapter three, you will read about an extensive list of water systems when you live off-grid, their different advantages and disadvantages, and how you can set them up yourself.

In the city, when you turn the faucet to wash your hands, bathe, or drink, you expect water to come forth automatically. You know it will come because that's the way things are set up where you live. Access to clean water in your home is a sure thing. However, collecting water will be an everyday part of your routine in other places far away from the city. And many times, clean water is very scarce.

In the Sahara desert, some women wake up before dawn each day to make their journey to collect water. Against the arid and brutal heat, they trudge on for miles until they reach the only nearby place with available water.

They then collect it by lowering and lifting their buckets into the holes in the ground. They become heavy with water but keep at it until they're finished. The water is often not even treated, as they don't have access to water filters made by modern technology.

In the wilderness, where bodies of water aren't always accessible, survivors have to collect water from plants or by digging in the ground. Unlike in the city, they can't just expect water to be available when they wake up in the morning. The water here also isn't sure to be clean, so it needs to be filtered somehow.

It's a constant part of their schedule each day because, without water, they can't survive. Many of us have experienced what it's like to have a water shortage. We realize simple things like taking a shower or making tea are things we might have taken for granted.

That's why you'll learn about the realities of collecting, cleaning, and maintaining your water systems when you start living off-grid. As you read this chapter, you'll learn about the various water systems you can choose from and how to set them up. You'll soon be ready to take on these projects and have a life as comfortable as you can imagine!

In ancient times, people had to provide for themselves. One main thing they needed was water. Humans are made of 80% water. The average time we can live without it is, at most, three short days.

Nowadays, many technological advancements and discoveries have made our lives infinitely easier and more prolonged. Still, many of the systems we use today originated hundreds of years ago from our ancestors, who have passed their knowledge down to us. One piece of knowledge they have taught us is rainwater harvesting. Rainwater harvesting is one way of collecting clean and drinkable water that we still use now!

While it's unknown which civilization performed it first, there is evidence of who practiced it. For example, there's a deep history of rainwater harvesting in the Middle East. The timeline goes all the way back to 2000 B.C. when people collected water from the hillside and stored them in Cisterns.

In ancient India, enormous reservoirs were developed to store rainwater. They still practice rainwater harvesting as systems have been built on top of their homes. In Northern America, they collected rainwater from the natural shape of the mountain and the water that would fall from it.

You see, as far back as ancient times, this has been practiced to supply everyone with water, one of the crucial things humans need. It's a tried and true system that has worked for centuries, and especially with our technology now, we can ensure our water is even safer than ever before.

According to the United States Environmental Protection Agency (EPA), the average American family uses 300 gallons of water a day. That isn't a typo. That's 300. Seventy percent (210 gallons) of that water is used inside the home and breaks down as follows ("How We Use Water," 2018):

- Toilet (24 percent)
- Shower/bath (20 percent)
- Faucets (19 percent)
- Washing clothes (17 percent)
- Leaks in the house (12 percent)
- Other (8 percent)

The other 30 percent (90 gallons) is used outdoors for washing cars and watering lawns. Needless to say, we use a lot of water.

That number can be cut down dramatically if you are responsible and conscientious. However, even if you can manage to cut that number in half, you still need a lot of water.

At a bare minimum, you'll want 500 gallons of water on hand at any one time. That's water that's already been pumped or collected and stored in a cistern or tank. If you can get more than 1,000 gallons and safely store them, that will make your life much easier. Storing water is crucial for survival and can also be important for other systems your house uses, such as heating.

CLEANING

Before we even get started on collecting water, we must talk about getting clean water.

Clean water is a serious problem in many parts of the world. Poor access to water, or water contamination, is a tragedy in the developing world. For most of human history, finding a reliable source of clean drinking water was very difficult and crucial. This is why ancient cities were always built on rivers for fresh water.

Water straight out of the ground or a pond will not be clean. It will have mud, clay, and a lot of other gross stuff you don't want to drink. Wherever you get your water from, you will need to include a filtration system—that includes rainwater. Water captured in barrels still probably touched a roof and gutter when collected. Even more, water in a barrel is a breeding ground for all kinds of things if it isn't treated.

The most significant risk is any form of contamination by microorganisms. If you ingest these, they can seriously mess up your guts. Water can also be contaminated by gas or contaminants leaking into the soil.

Do not drink unfiltered water. Water contains all kinds of microscopic organisms that will seriously harm you and potentially kill you.

Simply boiling water kills many different types of contaminants but not all. Most viruses and bacteria won't survive as they boil. Others can survive and can only be killed at a very high temperature, usually requiring a pressure cooker. Boiling may be a good enough solution for short-term survival, but boiling water in a pressure cooker is not a good long-term system.

Modern filters are so tight that the gaps in the mesh are measured in fractions of a micrometer. This means most microscopic particulates and organisms cannot get through it. It's also a great way of moving any kind of junk in your water. They usually contain a mix of ceramic and carbon, the same thing they use in the water filters that attach to your sink or use in a pitcher. Filters will need to be replaced periodically. Consult the instructions of any filter you use.

For your rain barrels, you might want to use tablets. Water-purifying tablets kill most biological invaders. Tablets usually use iodine, chlorine, or sodium, so you must be careful not to overtreat the water. You do not want to be consuming too much of the stuff that cleans the water. Purifying tablets also can't remove any harmful particulates, such as heavy metals.

Ultraviolet light can purify water by stopping microbes' ability to produce. Normal exposure to light can recontaminate the water. Light-treated water must be used shortly after cleaning or stored in a lightproof location.

If you have no access to water, you have probably chosen the wrong place to live. If, for some reason, you find yourself in a position where you only have access to saltwater, solar-powered desalination is an option.

In short, to get safe water, you will need one or more solutions to handle both biological and nonorganic junk.

RAIN

Rain is free, easy, and clean. It falls from the sky, and all you have to do is catch it before the earth drinks it. Setting up a series of rain barrels is the simplest way to do this.

You want to use any large surface area as a way to collect. Easy examples are the roof of your home as well as solar panels. The water can be caught using gutters and delivered into barrels. Just leaving a bunch of barrels out in the yard will not be very effective if you want to maximize the space to capture rainwater.

As mentioned earlier in this chapter, water stored in barrels needs to be treated. You absolutely do not want algae or mosquitoes making their home inside of it.

Rainwater is great, but it will not be enough for you. If you live in a very rainy environment and it's just you, you might be able to get away with it—probably not, though. For most people, especially those with children, rain barrels are a vital part of the water system, but they are not enough by themselves. Rain barrels are supplemental. They won't be the most important water source.

If you can, have the rainwater diverge directly into one of your main tanks. If you can't do that, you can manually add the water directly to the tank if you don't mind a little bit of heavy lifting. Rainwater can also be used as a gravity shower.

In the winter, your rainwater is now water derived from snow. If you heat it up, it will serve the same function. It's also much easier to collect because it's all over the place, and you can just scoop it up.

Believe it or not, harvesting rainwater is actually illegal in some places. Make sure you won't get a fine for catching water from the sky.

WELLS

If you're going to be living somewhere, you want a permanent, stable, and reliable water source—that means a well. For your main water source, digging a well is by far your best bet. Rain is fine if there's an abundance of it. Creeks and ponds might not be available or legal to take from. Delivery is fine temporarily, but it's not a permanent solution.

Shallow Well or Pump Well?

If there is water high enough, you may be lucky in that you can dig a shallow well. Basically, you need to get an excavator to dig out a big hole in the ground, about ten feet in diameter and around 18 or 20 feet in depth. If you're finding water at that depth, you are in luck. I'll keep saying it: Check your laws. Some pumps that go deeper than a precise number of feet are regulated. Yes, the laws are that finicky.

Once you have a hole, you can install the pipe, valve, and pump and run the pipe up over the top. Then, fill in the rest with gravel, then cover with dirt.

If you are feeling really rustic, you need water now but don't have electricity yet; or if you want a second, minor well, you can always use a lever hand pump—very old-fashioned but very effective for small amounts of water. Not a great way to get water for your whole house, but it's excellent as an intermediary step or a supplementary system.

Deep Well

One thing that's been a problem with settling up new land is finding locations to dig a well. It wasn't that long ago that con artists were making money using dowsing rods, wandering between the town, and promising they could detect places that were good for a well. Then he'd take their money and disappear before the people who hired them could realize their mistake.

Any piece of land that you want to dig a well on, you should investigate ahead of time. It would be a good idea to reach out and talk to the neighbors first. See if anyone else nearby has dug their own well. If none of them have, you might be able to speak with folks in the city about any records they have of natural resources. If you are going to need a well, you should use land where you are likely to find water.

Digging a well blind is extremely risky. If no other wells are nearby and you don't have good information on the water table, you are firing blind.

You may be able to find and create a relatively shallow well with just an auger and get very lucky. However, in some places, you need to dig and install pipes that are hundreds of feet down. Every single one of those feet costs a lot of money. Maybe you get lucky, and you find water 40 feet down. Maybe you don't get lucky and drill down 300 feet and still find nothing. The people who dig the well get paid whether they find water or not.

A well is probably your best source of water, but if you are not careful, you can end up spending a tremendous amount of money with no benefit. So be very careful.

Digging a well may be one of the most expensive projects to get your off-grid home up and running. However, on the plus side, adding a well will greatly raise the property value. As long as you did it with a company following all the rules and licenses, the well should pay for itself in value added to the land if you ever decide to sell.

Springs, Rivers, and Creeks

If you find a river or creek on your land, you may feel like you have an excellent water supply. We hate to break it to you, but many states do not allow you to draw water out of creeks, rivers, and ponds crossing through your land. That makes it illegal to draw water from a naturally occurring source. This is doubly true out west. Where water is especially scarce, they have appropriative water rights.

That creak, stream, or river you have potentially crosses through somebody else's lawn on its way to some other larger body of water. It would be seriously uncool to interfere with that stream that crosses into someone else's land. That's why you can't just build a dam and divert the water in another direction. That messes with someone else's property.

If you were grabbing some 100 gallons a year, you might not get caught, but we do not recommend breaking state law to get water when there are other ways to do it. You may have to enjoy the calming and serene bliss of the water, but tragically, you won't be able to take a shower with it.

Delivery and Pickup

In survival training, they will teach you that you can go three hours without shelter, three days without water, and three weeks without food. We need to upend that rule a little bit on our priorities. To get water, we need to pump. To get a pump working, we'll need electricity, so electricity is actually more important than water.

If you're developing an area with a hill, you can make things easier by putting water cisterns on top of the hill and running a line to your house, trenching it, and burying it underground. Natural gravity will give you natural water pressure without requiring any extra electricity.

When you first start your off-grid home, it may be a while before you can get access to your own water. You may be reliant on water from outside. If you have tanks set up and buried, with valves and pumps installed and pipes going to your home, you can hire a truck to deliver water and fill up your tanks. If not, you can go to the store, pick up as much as you need, and drive it back.

This is not a good long-term solution to your water problems. This is just costing you gasoline and time, plus the water is more expensive than if you were on the grid. You can rely on this kind of water supply for a short time while getting your permanent water system fully operational. Also, if there's some kind of problem down the road and you need to repair your system or something gets funky, you can get the water delivered if it's your last resort.

We only include it in this book because, realistically, you will be using delivered water for a short period at the start of your off-grid homesteading.

Storage

Water needs to be stored. You won't be pumping water every time you turn on a faucet. Water is pumped and stored in tanks as needed. Your indoor water is drawn from the tanks. The bigger the tanks, the more water you have at the ready. You want large volumes of it ready to go.

Like with everything else, if you want to be prepared and have more than you need, get it now because you might need it later.

Tanks and cisterns should be stored underground. After just a few feet into the earth, the ground is cool but not frozen. This is important because in the summer, an underground tank or cistern will not overheat and cause the water to boil, and in winter, it won't freeze or burst.

Any kind of pumping system will also need to be underground, including the valve. Like with the water, you do not want any part of the pump to freeze—that would be a major disaster. How much water you'll need and how big your tank is will depend on your personal needs, but we always recommend getting more than you need just to be safe.

Water collected from rain can always be added to your tanks to top them off and give your pump a break.

Key Chapter Takeaways

- **Lesson #1: The Importance of Clean Water**

Once you begin collecting your water, you'll need to find a way to clean it. Ensuring the cleanliness of your water will prevent many diseases you can get from unfiltered water. Knowing how to filter and prevent such things will allow you and your family to stay healthy as you live off-grid.

- **Lesson #2: Different Ways to Collect Water**

The main systems you can use to collect water as you live off-grid are rain barrels, cisterns, and various kinds of wells. Some of these you can set up on your own, but with others, you may need assistance from licensed professionals.

- **Lesson #3: Laws & Bodies of Water**

Many times, bodies of water near your off-grid home will have laws prohibiting you from collecting from them. Knowing the laws in your area and ensuring that the body of water is safe to take from will make things much easier.

- **Lesson #4: Delivery & Pickup of Your Water**

In the beginning stages of living off-grid, you won't automatically have collected water at your disposal. Knowing how to order and pick up enough water for you and your family will help you prepare for the coming weeks ahead.

- **Lesson #4: Storing Your Water**

Once you collect your water, you must find a way to store it so you won't waste a drop and can use it in the long run. Some ways to store them are in your rain barrels, cisterns, and tanks.

A Hands-On Approach to Your Learning

We know there are different types of learners, and reading and researching may not be as effective for some people. That's why we encourage you to come and book a call with us as soon as possible.

You'll reach your goals faster than you could alone and accelerate your learning to finally be independent. Your journey doesn't have to be so confusing and complicated, as we'll be your guide every step of the way.

Off-Grid Water Reliance Check-in Exercise

Before we proceed with the rest of the book, let's first explore where you are right now in your Off-Grid Journey.

Below, rate yourself on a scale of one to five on how accurate the statements are for you - a score of one means "not accurate," and a score of five means "very accurate."

After you have rated yourself according to the statements, add the sum total of your scores, then read "What Your Score Really Means" to determine the outcome of your results.

Check-in Statement	Rating
I am still reliant on the city's water systems.	

I have selected a water system for collecting water.	
I know **where** to collect water from and how to clean it.	
I have a budget plan for my water collection system.	
I know the primary systems I can use to collect water.	
I know the laws in my area and ensure that the body of water is safe to take.	
I know what to build for a steady running water supply in my home.	
I know how to order and pick up enough water to help me prepare for the coming weeks ahead.	
I know the advantages and disadvantages of each water system option.	
I know the proper way to store water so I can use it in the long run.	
I have a working, foolproof, dependable water system in my home.	

TOTAL SCORE:	

What Your Score Really Means

Score: 0 - 15

Reviewing Stage is Needed

With this score, you might have difficulty understanding how water management works. The function of water systems and how to set them up will be crucial because you'll need them daily. Clean, running water will allow you to do your daily tasks, cook, and hydrate, all of which are needed for your survival. Since it's all up to you, you have to be more hands-on and further review the things you have to know.

Score: 16 - 30

Ready to Choose Your Water System

You are well on your way to really getting the hang of things. Once you finally choose your water system, you're one step closer to a more self-sufficient life. Now, your job is to set everything aside and decide how you want your things to be.

Score: 31+

Prepared to Set Things up

You have already done what's necessary to overcome the lack of know-how for certain things. Now, it's time for you to take the next step. After you've chosen a system to set up at home, it's time to review how you will do so.

For some water systems, you won't need an extra pair of hands to set things up, but when building specific ones, such as a well, you'll have to navigate what you can or cannot do.

CHAPTER 4: GENERATING OFF-GRID POWER

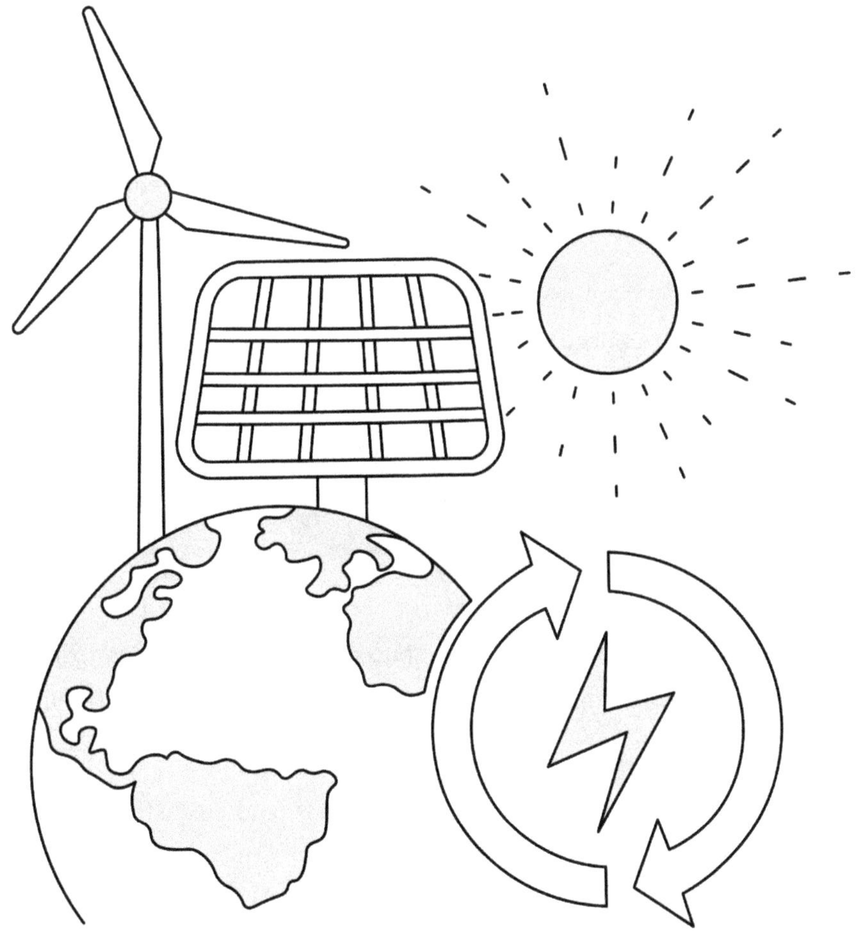

Chapter four lays out information on one of the most complex systems for living off-grid: electricity. You'll learn about the various types of power sources for electricity, how solar, wind, and geothermal power works, and how to set them up yourself.

As centuries pass, we can now experience the splendor that this discovery has brought. We can live in the comfort and privilege of a warm home, using our daily gadgets, and having light available whenever we need it!

Imagine a home without any power at all! Not only would it be a pain, but you wouldn't be able to use any of the appliances or gadgets you need daily for chores and work. When you live off-grid, you'll need to learn how to set up your power systems. Living comfortably and off the grid is possible with more knowledge gained. Throughout this chapter, you'll learn exactly what you need to do to power your future home.

Solar energy has been used by our ancestors as far back as 5BC. One of the first ways it was used was to light fires using a combination of glass and the sun that reflected through it.

North American Anasazi people even practiced keeping their homes warm by designing their homes to face the sun, which today would be called a passive solar architectural design.

Many discoveries about solar energy were made during the 16th and 17th centuries. But everything truly started taking shape when Edmond Becquerel discovered the Photovoltaic effect or light energy in 1839.

Many new inventions were created afterward until 1954, when Bell Laboratory finally created silicon solar cells that could transform sunlight into electricity! While it could only power small appliances at that time, this was when solar energy was revolutionized.

Decades later, Congress passed the Solar Energy Research, Development and Demonstration Act of 1974 to allow solar power to be more affordable and feasible for the masses.

Nowadays, more and more people are using solar energy because of how much of a sustainable and clean resource it is compared to our traditional ways of getting energy. It is important because it's one of the most sustainable ways to collect and use energy.

Thanks to our ancestors and scientists who have made this possible, solar energy is even more affordable today! And now, living off-grid is more viable than ever. With solar energy, we'll be able to have all the comforts that modern technology allows in more sustainable ways!

Power Sources and Saving

Renewable energy has come a long way but isn't a fully mature technology. Like everything in life, there are trade-offs. They have pros, and they have cons.

Solar and wind power can generate a tremendous amount of energy when the sun and wind are at their peak. This is great except for one big problem: They create more energy than is needed. The surplus energy can't be stored safely because battery technology hasn't been able to keep pace. When the solar panels aren't catching the sun or when the wind isn't blowing, they produce nothing. We need energy when we need it, not just when nature provides it.

Living off-grid means living on an electrical budget. On a municipal scale, this means that green energy still has to be supplemented with other energy, be it nuclear or coal. On a smaller scale, you can be flexible enough to make it work. You will want to get a reasonable estimate of how much energy you need. If you can get an estimate of how much you are using now, you can get a sense of how much energy production you will need in your off-grid home.

1,000–1,500W is probably enough juice for your needs, but everyone's needs differ.

The power source you use will depend on your environment. The more you can mix your energy sources, the better. If one isn't generating, another one might be able to make up the difference. The diversity of energy is reliable energy.

Naturally produced energy is about living on nature's schedule. When it offers wind or sun, you take it while you can get it. If you are using naturally produced power from wind and solar energy, you are living on an electrical budget. You have to regulate your own energy use because you can just use as much as you want and pay a bill for it later.

One way of handling this is by using the power when you have it. This is called "opportunity usage" and is a very effective way to maximize your power. Schedule all your heavy electrical activities for when the sun is up and the wind is blowing, and there will be no wasted energy. If you have a washing machine, a dryer, and a sunny day, that would be an excellent time to do your laundry.

SOLAR

Solar energy is cheaper and more readily available now than ever before. It's so common that it's no longer unusual to see solar arrays attached to the roofs of someone's home. Solar panels are made of crystalline silicon wafers. Contact with sunlight causes electrons to move about inside of them, and this flow of electrons is what generates an electrical current.

Big solar farms optimize their energy to follow the sun by turning the panels automatically to always face the sun and have the optimal angle with maximum coverage of the surface area of the panels. This is exactly how sunflowers operate—they always move to face the sun so they can get as much sunlight as possible.

Not all solar panels are equal. Some people simply lay them flat on the ground—which is actually the least effective way of catching the sun's rays. It'll be great at high noon during the summer when the sun is directly above it, but it will be increasingly useless as the sun goes down.

Higher-end models can do what those major industrial solar panels do and follow the sun. They are definitely more expensive, but they may be worth the initial investment if you can get more juice out of them and optimize your array.

Most people find that installing panels on the roof of their home is the smartest option depending on how they face the sun. Many people set up arrays on towers about the property, in areas without any shade or trees blocking them. Very often, the best place to put your solar array is in the garden for the same reasons. It's an open space with lots of sunshine.

You can't make a solar panel system without some electrical skills. If you know something about wiring up an electrical system or are willing to learn, you can do it yourself. However, it can be risky if you are inexperienced. Faulty craftsmanship can damage some of the systems and cost you money and time.

Building your own system takes planning and research. As stated many times in this book, always check out your local regulations. Some places require permits or official qualifications.

Solar panels also need to be weatherproofed. After they are put up and joined together, they need to be sealed so that water and moisture do not get into them. Make sure that any panels you purchase are from a reputable supplier and manufacturer. Getting cheap panels from an untrustworthy supplier could result in a fire. Look around. If something seems so cheap that it's too good to be true, it is. Safety first.

You can build solar panels from scratch out of individual solar cells if you like. It's not too difficult. You start by creating a backing for the panel. You can use a wooden board, and you will need to drill holes in the right place so that wires from each cell can pass through the back. They are then wired together using a soldering iron. They should be attached to your backing individually so they can be removed individually. If a single solar cell is damaged, it should be relatively easy to remove the single damaged cell and replace it without having to replace the entire thing.

A solar panel by itself doesn't do anything without an electrical system. You need to pair your panels with an inverter to turn the direct current (DC) into an alternating current (AC). Nearly everything you use requires AC power. Running DC into that stuff will not work.

Before you even begin designing your system, you should probably get a sense of how much power you will need. Look at your current electrical bill, and you might be able to get an estimate of how much juice you are using. Then, look at weather reports to see how many days of sunshine you get on average in the area that you are building. With a little bit of math, you should be able to get a sense of what the scope of your solar system needs to look like.

For beginners, we recommend that you purchase solar panel kits that come with all the instructions included and all of the tools necessary to build your solar system. Good kits also include racking and a means of mounting your system. If you want to do it yourself but don't really know how, these kits are definitely a wonderful option.

'Racking' refers to installing it either on the ground or onto the roof. If you are using an RV, then you will need to mount it on that. Whichever method you use, these must be very secure; you don't want them falling off or getting blown away by a gust of wind. Getting your solar panels from the same place you get your racking supplies might be a good idea to guarantee they will fit together. Even though some companies promise compatibility, these things can sometimes be like blue jeans. The size on the label says one thing, but when you actually try it on, you find it isn't quite what was promised.

Working with a professional who is a trained electrician with expertise in solar panel installations will likely be your best bet. They know all the laws and regulations, they are experts in their field, and they will probably get it right the first time. If you are a DIY person who knows a little bit about electricity and is willing to learn a lot more, this can be a great project for you to take on yourself. Letting a professional deal with it is a good call if you don't feel up to it.

Catching the sun won't be reliable for those living in places like the Pacific Northwest of America or Scotland. You can keep adding panels, but adding other energy sources is better.

Wind

The wind is a great option if you live out in the open in a windy place like Argentina, Perth, or Wyoming. If you live deep in the woods, you might not get enough wind to make it worth your while. Trees do a great job of breaking up the wind and shelter you from hurricanes and dangerously forceful winds. Unfortunately, it also means you can't get wind power.

Wind turbines are commercially available, but they aren't cheap. Some can generate as much as 3,000W—emphasis on CAN. Like solar power, just because the box says it can generate a large wattage doesn't mean it will. Nature makes that decision.

A lot of areas do not like the look of windmills, and regulate them. Like everything else, check the laws to ensure you're allowed to have them.

Windmills also need to be mounted on poles. Usually, higher is better, as there is less obstruction from your buildings, hills, and trees. Around 20 feet should do the trick in most cases.

GEOTHERMAL

Geothermal is a very cool option but has one major drawback: Getting it up and running can be very pricey.

Geothermal energy is not actually producing electrical power. It just makes heating and cooling easier and more efficient.

Geothermal works by drilling a deep hole in the earth and running water through it. The deeper into the earth you go, the less affected it is by the temperatures on the surface. In effect, the temperature is stable.

When it is ferociously hot outside, the temperature deep in the earth is cooler. When it is intensely cold outside, the temperature on the earth is warmer.

The more you want to change the temperature, the more energy you need. It takes more heat to make ice into a gas than it does to turn water into a gas.

Geothermal works by splitting that amount of energy by meeting your energy needs halfway. If you need to cool things down, the geothermal temperature gets you halfway from hot to cold. If you need it warmer, then it's the same thing.

It is very simple, practical, and, most importantly, reliable.

This is highly recommended. It doesn't provide electricity, but it makes your electrical systems much more efficient for heating and cooling your home and water.

MICRO-HYDRO

This is a very interesting option if your spot has running water. Unlike solar and wind, a moving river or creek is always moving. Depending on the time of year, you'll get more or less power, but it's always there for you if you need it.

Reach out to the Geological Survey or Department of Agriculture. They may have data on the speed and force of the water moving through your property. Hydropower might not be worth your time if it isn't strong enough. If your water source does produce enough force, like every other improvement on your land, you should contact whatever local department is in charge of energy or natural resources and ask them about the rules for diverting water.

If you have a green light for those two items, you'll need a generator, turbine, and piping. Consider yourself lucky because this is not an option available to most people living off the grid.

GAS-POWERED GENERATOR

A generator isn't anyone's first choice, but it's important to include. It uses gasoline—which is expensive and a pollutant—it's loud, and it smells bad. That said, you're going to want one.

You may need a generator to get by while getting yourself set up. You will need something until your other power sources are up and running.

It's important to have a generator in case of emergencies. Even if you seldom need it, you'll be very happy to have it when you do. As discussed earlier, several overlapping redundancies are crucial. You'll want a generator just in case. If you accidentally leave your keys in your truck overnight and drain your car battery, you will be very grateful to have a generator.

Important note: Gasoline goes bad. Gas is perishable. It has a shorter life span than you might realize. If you have a spare plastic tank of gas, you will need to change it out periodically. Pure gas that is properly stored can last six months. Gas blended with ethanol lasts three months, so keep this in mind. You don't want to fill a tank with bad gas.

There are options for petroleum-based stabilizers to add to gas, which will extend its life to one to three years.

If your gas looks too dark or you see any sludge in it, it is old, and you can't use it. Putting old or contaminated gas can ruin the machine you're trying to power.

Storage

Energy storage is going to be necessary because the wind won't always be blowing, and the sun won't always be shining. To store energy, we have two main options.

The obvious answer is batteries. There are lots of options, and not all batteries are created equal. You can get heavy acid batteries, the kind that is used in golf carts. Those are a fine option and are relatively cheap, although they are heavy and filled with acid, and you do not want to tip them over because they are full of liquid. You can also find lithium batteries, the same type used in smartphones. These are cheaper but also more expensive and often have less capacity.

Obviously, you'll need an electrical system to build these batteries and pull power from them when needed into any other electricity you are using in your home.

Battery storage is measured in amp-hours. That means a 100-amp hour battery will give you 100 amps for one hour... sort of. Batteries also have a natural discharge rate. This is called Peukert's law, which complicates the math a little. Batteries have different discharge rates that will also affect how much juice you get out of them. People who know a lot about this will check batteries for Peukert's exponents.

The discharge rate can also be affected by the temperature and the battery's age. This is all complicated stuff, and it actually isn't that important. You don't need to calculate the exact amounts of storage you need. You need to get a rough estimate of what you need and then add on a little bit extra just to be safe.

Energy can also be stored in water as it is very conductive. This isn't energy you can convert into electricity, but you are effectively storing thermal energy by heating water. When the sun is shining, and you are pulling in a lot of power from your solar arrays, this is a great time to channel some of that energy into your water heater. Tanks with hot water will stay hot for a while. As we discussed, you will be pulling more energy in than you need at that time and more than you can store for later. Heating your water during the day is the perfect opportunity to store energy in the water.

KEY CHAPTER TAKEAWAYS

- **Lesson #1: Off-Grid Power Sources**

Your source of electricity when you live off-grid will be quite different because you'll be relying on renewable energy. Your choice of energy sources will also greatly depend on the location's environment and weather conditions.

- **Lesson #2: Saving on Power**

As you live off-grid and rely on renewable energy to power your home, you'll need to make certain adjustments. Because your power source will rely on the wind or sunlight, there will be times when there's more/less power than usual. So regulating your energy according to that will help you make the most out of the power.

- **Lesson #3: The Best Options For Renewable Energy**

There are many sources of energy to power your home. Some of these are solar, wind, geothermal, and micro-hydropower. A gas-powered generator is often used as a backup if ever these fail to give electricity.

- **Lesson #4: Storing Your Power**

Storing your energy is crucial because you won't always have the light or wind to help give power to your home. Using a special and appropriate kind of battery will allow you to enjoy electricity in your home even when the weather conditions don't allow it.

Don't Be Held Back by the Technical Aspects

Powering your off-grid home is a tremendously difficult task. You'll have to research and decide on your power source, learn how to set it up, and have some knowledge of maintenance as well.

For some of us, we could get put off just from realizing the amount of work we'll have to do. But the thing is, you don't have to do it all on your own. Why not get a team of experts who can make things infinitely easier and faster for you?

Off-Grid Power Sources Check-in Exercise

Before we proceed with the rest of the book, let's first explore where you are right now in your Off-Grid Journey.

Below, rate yourself on a scale of one to five on how accurate the statements are for you - a score of one means "not accurate," and a score of five means "very accurate."

After you have rated yourself according to the statements, add the sum total of your scores, then read "What Your Score Really Means" to determine the outcome of your results.

Check-in Statement	Rating
I know about different renewable energy sources.	
I know the different power sources I can choose from to power my off-grid home.	
I have chosen a power source for my off-grid home.	
I have estimated how much power I need for my home.	
I have a budget plan for purchasing and setting up my off-grid power systems.	

I know how I will store my power.	
I am aware of the laws and regulations on off-grid power.	
I have knowledge of ways to save power for living off-grid.	
I know the advantages and disadvantages of each power source.	
I know what I need to plan and purchase for the different power sources.	
TOTAL SCORE:	

What Your Score Really Means

Score: 0 - 15 **Power Your Understanding**

Setting up power in your off-grid home is one of the trickiest things to master. Right now, your knowledge of it still needs to be polished, so the best thing to do is go over the chapter again. You should also research the power system you're most interested in.

Score: 16 - 30

Reassess Your Needs

You may have learned nearly everything you need to set up your power system, but you still feel as if you're at a crossroads. When this happens, you need to reassess your needs and what you can do. You might be feeling overwhelmed, and you need to take things step by step. Rethinking the necessities and focusing on those will help you continue without as much confusion.

Score: 31+

Begin to Set Up Your Power System

Now that most of your decisions are set and done, nearly the hardest parts are over. But now, you can use more hands-on experience for this stage in your journey. Since you know the items and resources you need, you can begin setting up your power system. It won't be easy, but knowing how to go about it step-by-step will make things much easier.

Chapter 5: Off-Grid Nutrition

In chapter five, you'll discover ways to supply yourself with nutrients once you live off-grid, including growing your food, raising livestock, the best foods to stock up on, and ways to preserve and store your sustenance.

You look past your window to the wide splendor of a garden. Your harvest for the year is slowly growing, vivid hibiscus and hollyhocks sway to the wind, and your apple and lemon trees are steadily sprouting hearty fruit.

You take out your tools, put on your boots, and as you step outside, you stroll across the field. The sky is crisp and clear blue. The smell of the air is sweeter from the fragrant flowers dotted along your feet.

You harvest the food that's ready: the potatoes, beans, basil, carrots, and leeks. You realize you have more than enough to eat as you begin thinking about all the recipes you can cook. After tending to your garden, you visit your hens to see freshly laid eggs.

You collect each of them and clean up your coop. You plan on making scrambled eggs for breakfast. After you're done with the morning tasks, you admire your own paradise, one you made with your own hands!

This picture of life doesn't have to stay in your imagination because this paradise can be real in a world where food shortages happen. Sometimes people have no way to take care of themselves except to depend entirely on unstable systems.

Knowing how to grow your own food and provide for yourself and your family is one more step to complete self-sufficiency. Soon, you'll learn how you can supply yourself with the necessary nutrients, be prepared, and even have your personal paradise.

We live in an increasingly industrially reliant culture. A culture that relies on fast food, disposable goods, and wasteful materials—a culture that is quickly consuming itself. But a set of agricultural systems throws this way of life out of the window. This is *permaculture*, a movement created to promote a sustainable and independent lifestyle.

It all began in the 1970s with ecologists and coworkers Bill Mollison and David Holmgren. They realized the growing damages of the Industrial Revolution and its impact on our culture, so they created permaculture. Through their studies, they discovered how nature goes through sustainable cycles without the help of man. They then were able to live in and teach their philosophy to others.

There is also another man, Masanobu Fukuoka, who has slowly built a following in this movement. He endorses a natural way of farming, where you disrupt the soil only to a minimum. Instead of weeding, he chose to flood his fields with water, which helped weaken the weeds. They were trimmed if necessary, but as much as possible, he let them grow.

Another voice in this movement is Ruth Stout, who advocates mulching plants with twigs, pulled weeds, leaves, and more. She also promotes no-till gardening, and many have followed her ideas.

From its humble beginnings, it's evident that permaculture has evolved into a revolutionary change. More people can now learn and apply these revolutionary teachings to create a healthier life for themselves. As we depend more on sustainable agriculture, we'll be more independent from using unreliable sources.

This movement promotes a sustainable lifestyle and also interdependence with community members. As you plan to live off-grid, you can learn infinite lessons from these mentors as you start to grow your own food and become self-sufficient.

Eating seems to be one of the most popular topics and for a good reason: People love food. Plus, when you grow your own food, you have a more personal relationship with it. It's one thing to go to the store and pick up a zucchini; it's another thing entirely to grow that zucchini yourself from start to finish, see the final product, and then prepare it and feed it to yourself and other people.

A lot of people are very concerned about their food. What you eat is very important, and if you are especially alert about these things, there is no better way to know what you are eating than to be the person who grows it. Large agricultural corporations have earned themselves a bad reputation due to their practices of using pesticides and genetically modifying their crops. It's no surprise then that organic markets and farmers' markets have become so popular.

GROWING FOOD

GARDENING

You're certainly going to want a garden. A garden is a fantastic option if you aren't using a full-scale farming operation. To maximize the value and productivity of that garden, we strongly recommend that you build a greenhouse. Greenhouses are less challenging to make than you might expect and have a few significant effects.

A garden inside of a greenhouse is less vulnerable to animals. If built correctly and securely, you won't have to worry about foxes and rabbits sneaking in and eating your greens.

Plants prefer warmer environments. The greenhouse contains both heat and moisture so that the plants are warm without drying out. The roof and walls protect the plants from the elements. Some plants are very sensitive to heavy rainfall, and several days of bad rain could wreck a garden. What you are growing ultimately depends on what the optimal temperature is. If you are going to be growing several plants at once, make sure that their optimal temperature overlaps so that all of them can be happy.

You want to keep the greenhouse relatively humid, but try not to break the 90 percent mark. Too much humidity could lead to mold. Likewise, if things get too cold at night, humidity can turn to frost and freeze your plants, so ensure that you are maintaining the heat during the night as well.

Every garden should have a few staple items. For a beginner, it's best to stick with plants that aren't too needy. Since you can maximize the heat and water levels, the greenhouse will extend the natural planting season, and you will be able to get more food in one year than you normally would otherwise.

Vegetables that aren't a terrible amount of work include:

- Any kind of hardy root vegetable, including carrots
- Basil
- Oregano
- Tomatoes
- Onions
- Garlic
- Cucumber
- Zucchini
- Lettuce
- Spinach
- Bell peppers
- Celery

The French chefs reading this book probably noticed that all of the ingredients for mirepoix are present. Many Cajun chefs also noted that the Louisiana variation, "holy trinity," is also included on the list. Needless to say, you know you are off to a good start.

A garden that you plan on living off of is a garden that produces all the things that you need to live—that means proteins, fats, antioxidants, and carbohydrates. Skipping out on any of these is not healthy.

If you're making a garden to survive, nutritional values can be the most important thing. Your staples will include:

- Potatoes
- Carrots

- Beans
- Squash
- Tomatoes
- Onions
- Corn

You want to mix and match your garden with foods that take little time to grow and also those that grow quickly. Then you can overlap their cycles and produce a constant set of nourishing plants.

Some of the plants that have a short harvest cycle include:

- Carrots
- Kale
- Spinach
- Beans

All of these will grow to full size within one to two months generally. Potatoes can take three to four months if you use a spud from some of your older potatoes.

Vegetables don't last long. As soon as you pick them, their clock starts ticking. If you plan on doing a full harvest so that you can replant all of them, make sure you have a plan to consume them or at least a plan to store them. Effectively storing them will be covered later in this chapter.

If you can, you should also get a few herbs growing. A bit of herb goes a long way, and you can grow most of them easily. Basil, rosemary, sage, parsley, and thyme are all relatively simple and are excellent in food when fresh if you haven't tried them before.

The first part of running a garden is learning how to do it and getting it set up. The nice thing about plants is that most of the growing they do doesn't require much help from you. They do all of the work as long as you put them in a good environment with good soil, water, light, and the right temperature.

If you want to get really fancy, you can integrate a greenhouse automation system. This requires a little bit of tactical know-how, but it will save you quite a bit of work in the long run.

By running pipes through your garden with small holes in it, with a time valve, you can have the garden automatically watered. After the programmed period, water will automatically pump through the pipes and sprinkle the water out of the tiny holes, provided that you put the pipes in the right places. This automatic valve mechanism can be controlled via the computer.

Another way to use computers is by ventilating your greenhouse. The temperature inside the greenhouse can't get too hot. Plants like hot temperatures, but they have their limits. Using a computer to check the temperature and automatically turn on a fan to start ventilating the greenhouse is a great way of letting a machine do the micromanagement for you.

If you have a greenhouse, that's excellent, but if your garden is going to be too large to put in a greenhouse or you don't want a greenhouse for whatever reason, you are going to need to protect your garden from critters that will want to go in there and enjoy your snacks. Putting any kind of fencing around it so that rabbits and deer don't just wander in and enjoy themselves at your expense is necessary.

RAISING ANIMALS

Chickens

Chickens are great. Chickens will produce an egg every other day or so. The daily recommended minimum for protein consumption is about 50 grams. An egg contains about six grams of protein. So a breakfast of three eggs will contain about one-third of your daily required protein intake.

For chickens, you will absolutely need to build them a chicken coop. This usually entails an area fenced in with chicken wire with a little indoor home for them to sit comfortably. You can also let them out during the day—they know where their home is and will return. They'll love to look for bugs on your lawn, but you don't want them out all the time because they are delicious treats for predators in the wild.

There is so much support and information out there. There is an increasing interest in raising chickens or even ducks at home. You can find lengthy tutorials on how to raise these animals online. Even in places like Detroit, a lot of people have taken up urban farming projects and created chicken coops in the middle of the suburbs. Now is a great time to get into small-scale chicken farming.

Chickens are very stupid and like to use their water as a bathroom. Change the water to make sure they don't kill themselves like that.

Chickens are great for laying eggs, but let us never forget that chickens are also great to eat. If you are raising organic, free-range chickens, you will get a very different product than what you might be used to at a grocery store. Your chickens will be considerably smaller but also way tastier. The ones you purchase at the store have been given growth hormones to make them huge; they get a little exercise and only "eat" rain. If you don't mind reducing your chicken consumption, you will have some extra tasty chicken as a reward.

A strange fact is that your chickens will seem to spontaneously die sometimes. You won't know why, and you can't afford a chicken autopsy. Don't be surprised when you come to your chicken coop and find that one of them didn't survive. That's just going to happen.

In any chicken coop, you will want one rooster. You do not want zero roosters, and you do not want two roosters. One rooster is exactly the right amount.

One rooster will be a good defender of the hens. The rooster will step in if anyone tries to mess with their hens. If there are zero roosters, the hens are out of luck.

If you put two roosters next to each other, they will fight. This isn't a guess—that's what roosters do. The underground animal fighting sport known as cockfighting will happen literally every time you put two roosters next to each other. Roosters love to fight, and they will peck each other to death. Putting two roosters together may as well net you zero roosters.

Fish

If you have a pond or you want to build a pond, you can stock your own fish inside of it. These should be purchased from a decent fishery. You want to make sure that your fish are disease-free so that they won't get each other sick and die. Also, depending on the breed of fish you are going with, you need to get the male-to-female ratio right. Otherwise, you might find it overpopulating too quickly, or you might find males fighting with one another depending on the species.

Your fish can be contained within a cage inside the pond, making it very easy to scoop them out with a net—not exactly like shooting fish in a barrel but very close.

Pigs

Pigs grow fast and will eat almost anything. They consume a lot of food, around six pounds a day, and will excrete one and a half pounds of waste. Since they'll eat almost anything, they will happily eat all of your leftover foods that are in table scraps, so they never have to go to waste.

Each pig will need at least 50 square feet of space and a pen you build for them. You must keep the food and water far away from each other, optimally at opposite ends of the pen. They tend to defecate near the water. If they start contaminating their own water supply, you're going to have to change it out. It's not good for them to be eating their own waste.

Pigs are very sensitive to sunlight. You can tell because they have very little fur and very light skin. You will definitely want to give them some kind of covering. Pigs usually protect their skin by rolling around the mud, but if they don't have mud because it is a particularly dry time or dry place, then they're going to need something else.

Once a pig has stopped gaining weight, usually at around 280 pounds or more, they are ready to eat. If you know how to butcher a pig or are willing to learn, that's great. Otherwise, you ought to contact a butcher who's close to you and who can do that job for you safely and properly.

Pigs are very smart and very friendly. Not the wild ones: They will fight you. However, domesticated pigs are very friendly. There's been a growing trend where people even adopt pigs as family pets, just like dogs, and if you have not spent time around pigs, you may be surprised.

People who did not grow up on farms when they first encountered farm animals have a very different experience. People who grew up around animals and are accustomed to killing them and eating them have a very deep understanding of what meat is and where it comes from. They don't have any illusions about it. When most urban and suburban people see a chicken nugget, they don't think about it as it is.

When you spend time with a pig that you mean to ultimately slaughter and eat, it is understandable if you become emotionally attached. Your experience with animals is probable to be either pets or vermin. When the time comes, you might not feel good about killing the animal. There's no special advice on this; we're just warning you that this is a possibility. You can power through the experience and really confront what meat is, or you can decide you can't do it.

Goats

Goats are wonderful for milk and don't take up nearly as much room as cows. Some people dislike goat milk, while others think it's great and are willing to pay a premium for it, which is why you may see goat milk and cheese at a higher price at the store. Goats are sensitive to wind and need shade access because they tend to overheat. Be sure to keep your goats in an environment where they can keep cool.

Goats are natural lawn mowers. They will graze all day and keep your lawn in great shape. They can eat several pounds of food for a day just from grass and any hay that you supplement their diet with. They can also drink several gallons of water, more or less, depending on how much grazing they do, since a lot of their water needs are satisfied by grass.

If you are going to build them a place to live, that's a fantastic idea. They will want a place to sleep and be safe from predators and a place to keep the sun off of them—these shelters should probably be 70 square feet minimum.

There are many things in nature that will poison your goat, which they don't know better than to eat. Things like poppies, stagger grass, and buckwheat are dangerous to a goat, so keep an eye on those.

Goats are also notorious climbers. Even domesticated goats love to climb things. A goat will even climb on top of other animals. Use an image search engine and look for yourself. Keep this in mind because if you have any way for the goat to get onto your roof, they might try to do that. If you are running solar panels on the roof, you probably don't want a goat walking around on them.

Rabbits

Rabbits are a classic option. Rabbits are perfectly fine, as are any other lean game, so long as you are keeping them part of a well-balanced diet. You cannot survive on rabbit meat alone, however. There's a concept called rabbit starvation, also known as protein poisoning, and it is caused by the overconsumption of protein with no fat, carbohydrates, or micronutrients.

Rabbits don't require a lot of space, which is nice. They are extremely good at escaping, though. Your rabbit cage needs to be tighter than Alcatraz; otherwise, they will get out. Rabbits are natural diggers, so you'll need to make sure that you have some caging on the ground or floor so they don't get out that particular way.

Also, rabbits are cute. If you get cold feet and do not want to butcher them, that's fine—you can always keep them as pets. However, don't let rabbit breeding get out of control, which is something that can easily happen if you aren't careful. Breeding is great if you're making food for stew, but it's not good when suddenly you have way more pets than you know what to do with. The same situation goes with pigs.

Turkey

Turkeys are an all-American bird, and you can purchase them from a turkey breeder or farm for very cheap. Turkeys are very sensitive animals, and you will likely lose several of the first few weeks after buying them. Chicks need to have a warming unit when they are young, such as 100–250W lamps. You need to keep the warming unit at about 100 degrees

Fahrenheit for the first week—they want to be toasty. After the first week, they are much less vulnerable, and you can gradually reduce the heat; after a few months, they won't need any heat at all.

Turkeys grow fast, and after three and a half months, they will be big enough that they are ready to be eaten. At 35–45 pounds, they produce a lot of meat, so be sure to have a way to store the meat properly or share it with others. There's a reason why a turkey is a traditional bird for Thanksgiving—many people sitting together can all share a meal together.

Turkeys are also very smelly. You do not want turkeys anywhere near your house or upwind of it. They also aren't terribly friendly. Unlike some of the other animals, they are not good pets, but they are good food.

Unlike pigs and chickens, there is no way you will get emotionally attached to a turkey. To be perfectly frank, they are mean, and their odor is very pungent. If you are squeamish about killing an animal, maybe a turkey is a good way to start because you will not feel bad.

Bees

If you have a sweet tooth, you could even consider raising bees. This is an insect that is absolutely vital to the ecosystem and great if you like sugar. Honey is the only known food that never goes bad. You don't need to do anything with a container of honey to maintain it. Honey never rots. Honey will retain its freshness longer than you will be alive.

Beekeeping is a very popular hobby. It also has two wonderful side effects: It will produce honey and pollinate your garden. The easiest way to get started with a beekeeping operation is to purchase the basic starter kits. These are not difficult to find on the Internet. A starter kit usually contains everything you need: frames, a hive feeder, a queen excluder, a smoker, and all your protective gear.

You can keep your bees within a quarter-mile of your garden, and they will do all the work of pollinating your plants. Also, where you place them can affect the flavor of the honey. Putting bees next to cloves will add a clove flavor to the honey.

It's a fun hobby and requires some research because there's more to it than you might think. Honey can also be a cool gift. Putting it in a jar and giving it to someone is a neat and personal thing.

Another by-product of raising bees is wax which can be used for sealing, protecting food to extend life, and making candles.

Dogs

No, we're not suggesting that you eat dog meat! You're not going to eat the bees, either. They are just included here because we're already discussing animals.

Dog people are lucky. An off-grid lifestyle is wonderful for dogs. They have tons of space to move around, and they don't need to be taken on walks because there's so much free space for them to roam around and nowhere for them to run off to.

Dogs also love spending time with people while working outside, which you will be doing plenty of. Dogs are essentially wolves that were genetically engineered through selective breeding to become home security systems. In a city, you'll find dogs barking at almost any noise that they hear. They bark at people walking by on the sidewalk or another dog a block away that is heading toward that sidewalk. Deep in the country, that response is essential. If you are isolated, it's unlikely that you will have unwelcome human visitors, but you can certainly expect unwelcome animal visitors. This could be foxes coming to eat your chickens, a bear simply wandering through, or a raccoon who has sniffed out your trash. Whatever it may be, dogs have an extremely sharp sense of smell in hearing and will know if you have visitors long before you do, and they will eagerly tell you about it.

FOODS TO GROW/STOCK UP ON

Food storage is crucial. Humans have developed many clever ways to keep their food clean and safe before refrigeration.

There are a few foods that are always good to have on hand. Even if you aren't living off-grid, having these in your home is smart.

RICE

Rice has a long shelf life, and if properly stored, rice can last six months or longer. If you also keep it refrigerated, you can get twice as much time out of it. Brown rice is an excellent source of vitamins and fiber. Brown rice is the most nutritious, and if you're eating it to stay alive, just go where the nutrition is.

Rice is a staple food for more than half of the planet. That's a pretty big endorsement.

BEANS

The best friend to rice is beans. This is a well-known and well-traveled survival food. It's also very versatile and can be used in a lot of different ways. Dried beans can be stored for a long time and can be hydrated rather quickly by soaking and heating them.

Beans are an excellent source of protein, and when complemented with rice, it forms a complete protein.

Nuts

They are an excellent source of protein and fat; dried nuts also store very well.

Cabbage

Yes, cabbage. It is low in calories but has a ton of nutrients, including B6 and C, and is very fibrous. It's also very versatile because it can be used in salads. If you are into pickling, you can turn it into sauerkraut or kimchi, a great flavor addition with a very good shelf life.

Corn

It's very easy to grow as long as the soil temperature stays high enough to allow for germination and you have mature soil.

Cucumbers

If you plan on pickling, you should have cucumbers. If you are just getting cucumbers for pickling, keep in mind that there is a specific type of cucumber called a pickling cucumber. The ordinary cucumber you're used to that you put on a salad does not work the same way, but you might also like regular cucumbers.

Potatoes

Everybody loves potatoes. It's a starchy crop that's high in carbohydrates, which is important for getting your calorie intake high enough. These are crops that you are trying to live off of, and calories are your body's fuel. Yukon Gold potatoes are probably the best choice.

Sweet Potatoes

Everything we just said about potatoes is true of sweet potatoes. They are calorie dense and have much higher iron content than your average potato. The leafy greens that grow on them are also edible. They have a longer growing season, longer than almost anything else you will be raising. However, sweet potatoes might be worth the extra time and effort if you like them.

Tomatoes

Setting aside the argument about whether it is a fruit or a vegetable, the tomato is a pretty easy plant as long as you give it ample water. They also like the temperature on the warm side. Tomatoes are great on so many things and can be turned into sauces, added to salads, added on top of burgers, and plenty of other applications.

Lentils

Lentils are packed with protein. It's very difficult to get a decent amount of protein from plant sources: Ask any vegetarian who is conscious of their nutrition. Lentils have around 18 grams of protein per serving—that is the same amount of protein as three eggs. Also, lentils are one of the oldest crops that humans have ever cultivated. It is ancient, and lentil soup is just delicious, so if you don't like lentils, start liking lentils.

Spinach

This plant is easy to grow and is packed with vitamins and minerals. For the adventurous, spinach can be stored by freezing it or dehydrating it and then crushing it into a powder. Now you have a powdered nutritional supplement available.

Berries

Everybody loves berries. Raspberries, cranberries, blueberries, or whatever kind of berry. They're all good. They have a lot of nutrition and natural sweetness, and you can do a lot with them. You can turn them into jelly and incorporate them into nearly any dessert item you can think of.

Dry Seasoning and Salt

There's no reason not to make your food taste good, even in an emergency or disaster. Always have seasoning; there's no good reason not to. Dried herbs and spices last a really long time.

Dehydrating, Salting, and Smoking

For food to go bad, it needs to be wet. Salting food increases the acidity and dries it out, making bacteria grow much slower. This is exactly why beef jerky was invented. Salted meats have been with humans for as long as we've had salt.

You should consider building a smokehouse if you really enjoy food and want to go the extra mile. The process of smoking food adds a wonderful flavor that's impossible to replicate and dries out the food as well, which helps preserve it. Smoked salmon, for example, is delicious and a fantastic source of protein.

You can dehydrate meats, but you can also dehydrate fruits. It's also a good idea to put a type of acid on it, such as lemon juice or another citrus, because the dehydration process takes a while. You want to prevent any bacteria from starting a home there during the process.

There are plenty of ways to dry food, including the inside of an oven, or you could have a special dehydrator that uses electricity. One good option is to use a non-electric dehydrator. It should take six hours minimum but can take a lot more depending on the thickness and what it is you are dehydrating. It's hard to measure exactly how much time you need to dehydrate any kind of food because, depending on your environment, it will change a lot. The outside temperature, humidity, and amount of wind passing through will greatly alter these times. With that being said, you should check in on your dehydration regularly.

Dehydrating doesn't need to use any electricity. Solar dehydrators are a great method that uses the sun to dehydrate. As long as you have a rack to place the food on, make sure that they are ventilated, they are stacked accordingly, and have netting around to keep any bugs off of it; it's not too difficult.

There are many different designs for this sort of thing—one is to create a flat box with a mesh to lay food on and then cover it with a metal covering. The sun will heat the metal, raising the internal temperature. This is a straightforward DIY method as long as there's proper ventilation underneath it to allow moisture to escape.

You can dehydrate beef and fish but DO NOT try to dehydrate birds or pigs. Exposing those kinds of animals to air for longer than is absolutely necessary is extremely dangerous. Do not do it.

Pickling and Canning

There's been a recent new interest in recreational pickling and canning. These are excellent ways to preserve food. Pickling also has the advantage of adding a vinegar flavor to whatever you want.

You can pickle or can just about anything, including meat. Things that are canned need to be adequately sealed, so double-check them. Once canned, they need to be appropriately stored in a cool place without too much sunlight. This could mean a pantry or shed. If you are in a warmer climate, you should consider building a cellar. The sun's heat doesn't penetrate very far into the earth, and if you dig down just a short way, you can make a permanently cool space.

If a cellar is too much, it is totally fine if you want to bury your food. A hole in the ground, covered up, will be a natural refrigerator and keep the sun off and hopefully away from animals.

COOLING

Some kinds of foods absolutely need to be stored in a cool place. Some can be left at room temperature; you probably know which ones are already. According to the FDA, certain foods will require refrigeration, and that temperature needs to be 40 degrees Fahrenheit or less. That's very close to freezing temperature. During the winter, you don't need to worry about this that much because if it is already 40 degrees and cold around, then nature is handling the refrigeration for you.

In the summer, you will need to find other ways of storing your meat, poultry, fish, dairy, certain cooked foods, eggs, and all the rest.

Certain foods you already know you can leave out are your coffee, bread, onions, honey, olive oil, and potatoes—these are all fine.

The oldest traditional method is to simply build a root cellar. A hole in the ground will be much cooler than the surface or the inside of your home during the summer.

You can always go with the old-fashioned route of getting a cooler if necessary. If you don't plan on ever storing your food for particularly long, some of the newer and more expensive coolers are extremely good at retaining cold temperatures.

If you make a mistake and don't do a good job of preserving your food, look for the following symptoms: nausea, diarrhea, abdominal pain, fever, and vomiting. If you are suffering from one or more of those symptoms, especially if other people in your home are after eating the same thing, you need to reach out and contact medical help immediately—you may be suffering from food poisoning. This can be very dangerous, as it's more than just a stomachache.

Whatever food preservation method or methods you use, don't take any chances with your own health. If food looks iffy, don't take risks.

A really nice, well-insulated chest freezer and/or refrigerator are great. They use less electricity than you might expect, just as long as you don't have kids who like to hang out with the door open, looking at everything in the fridge. Don't get a cheap fridge or freezer. A really great, well-insulated fridge pays for itself.

HOW TO FEED YOURSELF WITHOUT POWER

Electric ovens use a ton of energy. You cannot use an electric stove, as it is simply not realistic. Likewise, microwaves can be very power-hungry, too. They might be fine to use when you are running at peak energy intake, and you have sunshine and wind, but it's not a great method. Electric stoves are terrible anyway, so nothing is lost. There are plenty more electrically conservative cooking methods that are simply better for cooking.

WOOD STOVE

If you already have a wood stove in your house keeping you warm, why not cook on it, too? This is an ancient and rustic way of cooking food, but it served our ancestors well for hundreds of years. The same fire that's heating up your home also has a flat surface on top. You can simply put a pot on it or a skillet and do your best to control the temperature by controlling the fire. It's not using any more power than before, so there's no reason not to utilize it.

During summer, you probably don't want to be having a piping hot fire in your living room. Try to avoid that heat as much as possible; during the summer, you will want to stay far away from any kind of fire and try one of the other options.

Solar Oven

A solar oven is a box with mirrors on the inside and a couple of missing sides. Basically, it's a big shiny device that catches solar energy and then points it into a focal point inside of it. Whatever you want to cook, you simply place it inside the container at that focal point. This will heat up whatever you are cooking on a sunny day very quickly. Think about when you touch metal on a hot day and how hot that gets.

This type of cooking is probably not great for everything. It is excellent for anything that you need to cook slowly or something that doesn't need to be cooked at a high temperature. For example, you will not be cooking steaks or kebabs on one of these things. Instead, any kind of stew would be excellent, or any kind of vegetable that you can cook slowly would be a great way to go. This is a completely green, electricity-free slow cooker.

There's no way to turn the temperature up or down or to regulate it in any particular way, so your best option is to check on it frequently or to place it in a spot where, after enough time has passed, the shadow will cover it and essentially turn it off.

Propane

For cooking, you can use tanks of gas. This is just like a propane tank on a grill that you would use outside. The only difference is that it is a built-in device in your home and also contains an oven. You can't cultivate propane on your own land, which means you will need to purchase it elsewhere or have it delivered.

Gas is great for cooking and is the preferred heating element for the best chefs. It's also relatively cheap if you are just using it for cooking and not trying to heat your entire home with it.

Grilling

Just as simple as that: Everybody knows how to grill, and everybody loves grilling.

If you're using propane to grill, you'll need to have propane on hand. If you already happen to have propane running in your kitchen, that is very handy. If you are a charcoal kind of person, that is a great option. Charcoal doesn't go bad. You can store that for as long as you like.

Grilling means great flavor and outdoor tradition. With a large enough surface, you can prepare a lot of food at the same time. That makes it a great option if you have a lot of guests or a large family.

If you are raising pigs or you are doing any hunting, a pellet grill is a fantastic option for cooking large amounts of meat. Slowly add in little pellets of wood pulp—they look a lot like hamster food. This keeps feeding a fire at exactly the right amounts to maintain a steady temperature. You can get a slow cooking process going, then wait 12 hours, culminating in an unbelievably tasty and tender meal the next day, with very little effort.

Earth Oven

Earth ovens are excellent options. You need a slab of stone, and you're going to house that using rocks and dirt to create something like a mound with a mouth on one side that food could be inserted into. Beneath it, you can put in some lumber to burn. These things, once they're cooking, get ridiculously hot. If you pop an oven into this, your food will be fully cooked in just a few minutes. It is a very efficient way to insulate the heat, and very little gets wasted, even with the open side.

When you want to keep your home as cool as possible during the summer months, cooking outside is a great way to ensure the heat stays outside. You can cook food crazy fast. From a cooking and aesthetic frame, earth ovens are just cool.

They lend themselves to cooking certain kinds of food very well, which, if you are into cooking, is a fun culinary experiment. Also, they happen to be very easy to build. They're also very cheap because you mostly only need bricks and dirt. Anyone can make one with a few simple instructions.

Sun Oven and Outdoor Fires

You do not want to cook food indoors on a hot day. All the heat produced will just make your home that much hotter. Cooking outside is a great solution. It's no accident that summer is the grilling season.

Sun Oven is the perfect product to reduce indoor heat. It's a box with a couple of open sides and reflective surfaces inside. This works exactly as you would expect. The sun reflects and cooks whatever you place inside the Sun Oven. It's not fast—it works like a slow cooker, which makes it great for stews and chili.

LIVING OFF THE LAND

Depending on your environment and your personal ethics, you can do what people have done for millennia. Nature readily provides protein in the form of animals. Hunting is undoubtedly an option that you can avail yourself of if you want.

This isn't a book about hunting, and we won't go into deep detail about it, but if it is something you're interested in, there are plenty of resources available so that you can learn more about the topic.

States and counties have many hunting, fishing, and trapping laws, and you will need to learn them to not break any laws.

DON'T EAT WILD MUSHROOMS

This should go without saying, but some people don't know: Do NOT eat wild mushrooms. We cannot say this strongly enough. We don't care if you have a book on identifying mushrooms. Unless you are a mycologist, do not go putting wild mushrooms in your mouth. Mushrooms can be very dangerous. Even with photographs, the differences between a safe one and a dangerous one can be indistinguishable.

Also, don't eat berries. Don't eat things in the woods if you don't know what you're doing.

HUNTING

There are considerations about what kinds of animals you can hunt during which portion of the season. Hunting with a gun usually has a very short season. An average size buck can net you an average of 60 or 70 pounds of meat. A boar can net you double that, which is a lot of meat. You should have some friends over or a good way to store it.

If you're using more difficult means of hunting, such as a bow or a black powder rifle, you will have a larger season to hunt in.

If you live in a remote area that has dangerous wildlife, such as bears or cougars, having a form of self-defense might be very valuable. Bear spray and other nonlethal weapons are good to have, but if your concern is protecting yourself from a mama bear who feels threatened by you, you're going to want the best tool that you can avail yourself of. This can mean a 10mm pistol at your side or a strong hunting rifle chambered in something like 6.5mm Creedmoor.

Most animals are not interested in you and will not pick a fight with you. However, starving and desperate animals might take their chances; an animal that perceives you as a threat to their young might attack you. These kinds of attacks don't happen often, but when they do, they are brutal. People are torn apart, isolated in the wilderness, and unable to contact medical aid easily.

A well-placed shot will kill an animal so quickly that they are dead before they realize what has happened. Taking a bad shot and wounding an animal is a serious faux pas among hunters. Hunters do not want to hurt animals: They want to hunt animals. Wounding an animal is cruel, and tracking a wounded animal to finish the job is not anyone's idea of fun.

If you are interested in hunting but are not experienced, your best bet is to make friends with someone who is. There are a lot of things to learn, not just the laws, of which any good hunter will be well aware. There are many things you should familiarize yourself with before you go walking around in the woods with a gun and no idea what you are doing. There are also considerations, like how to safely harvest what you need, how to kill an animal most humanely, how to stay downwind of an animal, or how to transport it after being shot.

FISHING

Fishing is a great form of recreation, and the catch you get will be a great form of protein. If you have access to water that has edible fish, that can be a great asset. Depending on where you live, you might have fishing options all over. You aren't locked to your property, remember. There may be great lakes and streams close enough that you can walk or drive and get yourself a meal—with a fishing license, naturally.

For the truly committed fish eater, you can build an artificial pond and populate it with your own supply of fish. With a river, you can trap fish with zero effort and come by and pick them up as you like.

TRAPPING

Trapping is a tricky business but has been a staple for eons. Trapping doesn't mean those terrifying spiky metal claws, like bear traps. Those are illegal, so do not use them. If you have one, we don't know where you found one, but don't use it.

Trapping usually means cages and snares. Once again, this depends on local laws, and you need to research them before you get involved. The advantage of trapping is that you don't need to do anything other than set up the traps and visit them occasionally. This generates a passive supply of animals without the work of chasing.

It's simply pieces of twine that are attached in certain strategic locations.

If you are tracking, you may be able to find common routes for rabbits. If they find a path they like, they will keep using it, knowing it is a relatively safe trail. However, if you know about it, it is not so safe for them. A live trap or a snare in one of these spots could nab you a bunny.

If you are the kind of person that isn't squeamish about eating squirrels, just know that they are very easy to catch in a snare. Simply by taking a piece of wood and leaning against a tree, squirrels are lazy like all animals and take the path of least resistance. Squirrels always walk up the branch leaning against the tree, which makes a branch the perfect place to leave a snare.

Snaring and trapping is a game of numbers. The more traps you have set out, the more likely you are to catch any animal. Whatever traps you have on your property, you should check them a couple of times a day just to see if anything is there.

Snare traps are cheap, but live traps are easy. Simply get a cage that will close itself when something goes inside of it. Bait that with something the animal of your preference likes and visit to see if anyone took the bait.

KEY CHAPTER TAKEAWAYS

- **Lesson #1: Growing Your Own Food**

Because you will be practicing self-sufficiency living off-grid, you will also need to grow your own food. Through gardening, you will be able to produce fruits, vegetables, herbs, and more.

- **Lesson #2: Raising Livestock For Self-Sufficiency**

If meat is a big part of your diet, you should consider raising your own farm animals. The easiest animals to raise would be chickens, fish, pigs, goats, rabbits, turkeys, and even bees.

- **Lesson #3: The Best Food to Grow & Stock up on**

In case of emergencies, it's good to have food with long shelf lives which you can store and eat in case you run out of your other food. Some in this list are the easiest vegetables to grow, which will also help your strength and health.

- **Lesson #4: Eating Even Without Power**

Since there might be some minor setbacks sometimes, you might not be able to cook your food in the usual way. Even without electricity, some options to eat are using a wood stove, solar oven, propane, grilling, and earth oven.

- **Lesson #5: Other Ways to Eat Off-Grid**

Some other ways to have a source of nutrition are foraging, hunting, fishing, and trapping. You must also consider the laws in your area for these practices.

Become Self-Sufficient Easier Than Ever

While not everyone has a natural green thumb or a connection to animals like Dr. Doolittle, you can still discover ways to make it work for you. You don't need the talent to supply yourself with food once you live off-grid, but you certainly need to know what you're doing.

Off-Grid Nutrition and Homesteading Check-in Exercise

Before we proceed with the rest of the book, let's first explore where you are right now in your Off-Grid Journey.

Below, rate yourself on a scale of one to five on how accurate the statements are for you — a score of one means "not accurate," and a score of five means "very accurate."

After you have rated yourself according to the statements, add the sum total of your scores, then read "What Your Score Really Means" to determine the outcome of your results.

Check-in Statement	**Rating**
I have begun growing my own food in my garden.	
I have knowledge of how to grow my own food.	
I know the easiest vegetables to plant to get started.	
I know the vegetables with the shortest harvest cycles.	
I know the best foods to stock up on with the longest shelf life.	
I know the different ways to store and preserve my food.	
I know how to cook food in case there is no power.	
I have begun researching how to raise different livestock.	

I have decided to raise livestock.	
I know how to forage and do it often.	
TOTAL SCORE:	

What Your Score Really Means

Score: 0 - 15 **Feed Yourself With More Knowledge**

It's time to get serious about your off-grid venture so you can take care of yourself and your family. Making sure you and your family are well fed with the most amazing meals will make your home all the more enjoyable. All you have to do is to know more about gardening. Even if you're not planning to be completely self-sufficient by raising livestock, it would still do you good to have more knowledge on it.

Score: 16 - 30 **Take Your Skills to the Next Level**

Now that you have the knowledge to take care of yourself off-grid, you must start planning your practice. Even if you're not yet living off-grid, you can start small by planting vegetables in your backyard or even in pots in your apartment. If you put in the effort, it's possible to really get started even before the big move.

Score: 31+

Grow Your Self-Sufficient Garden

You are now at a point where you probably have sufficient knowledge on growing your own food and even raising livestock. Now it's time to improve your skills by planting even more.

Begin planting vegetables, fruits, herbs, and even trees! If you have decided on raising your own farm animals, you can start small with chickens by taking care of them, cleaning their coop daily, and having the benefits of fresh eggs. Remember, your knowledge won't be of any use until you actually put in the work.

CHAPTER 6: HEATING AND COOLING YOUR OFF-GRID HOME

Chapter six gives a spiel on the different possible choices for heating and cooling systems in your off-grid home, including the pros and cons of each, how they work, and how they can be installed.

Outside where the cold, harsh winds blow, or the scorching heat arises, we tend to retreat to our homes where warmth can envelop us or cool air from fans can soothe us. But when you live off-grid, things can get a whole lot stickier and chillier if you don't plan well.

We need a suitable place to stay safe and warm when winter comes. The climate can hurt our health if we're cold for too long. Some of the effects are worsening asthma attacks, arthritis, depression, and more ailments.

If you're able to plan and set up a sustainable heating system, your home can be a haven from the biting cold, where you can curl up with mugs of hot chocolate with your family.

As for the summer, you not only have to worry about cooling yourself but also your animals if you choose to raise livestock. When the heat is too much, our health can also be affected. Fevers, migraines, and even something as serious as a stroke can happen!

It's crucial that you find ways to stay cool in your off-grid home because you'll also have to do tasks outside your home. A cool breeze with a nice cold drink will help protect you against heat waves!

In this chapter, you'll learn how you can stay toasty and warm throughout the cold weather and refreshingly cool throughout summer days. Living off-grid and living comfortably don't have to be separate things. If you know what to do, your journey will be a pleasant and cozy one!

Geothermal energy has existed for billions of years, but archaeological evidence shows that the first human use of geothermal resources began around 10,000 years ago. In North America, Paleo-Indians encountered hot springs. Because of the heat and comfort they brought, they decided to settle there. They then used the hot springs as a source of warmth, bathing, and healing.

Further down the line, geothermal energy was put into industrial use in 1892 in Boise, Idaho. The residents here experienced the first-ever district heating system in the world. The heat from the hot springs was extracted as the water was piped from there to the town. This amazing heating system provided hundreds of homes with warmth, and to this day, this invention still makes its rounds.

It's known that geothermal heating is one of the best sustainable choices for those wanting to live off-grid. Now, looking back to the past and seeing the people who first used geothermal energy, we can see how significant it still is today because it can still serve its purpose incredibly well in this modern age.

Heating and cooling are easy to leave as afterthoughts until the moment you need them. You will be miserable if the temperature gets too hot or too cold. If it gets bad enough, it can be lethal. There are a lot of options here, which is nice.

To be perfectly honest, if a lot of things aren't going great, you can put up with it. If you have to haul your water out or if you can't get your garden running and have to go to the grocery store, you can still live with it. However, if you live in a home that is 95 degrees Fahrenheit for a week, you will most likely abandon this project as soon as possible. No one can be expected to live like that when there is a cozy Holiday Inn just 25 miles away.

If your temperature is off, everything else will be off, too, so this is one thing you definitely need to get right.

If you have animals, don't forget them! If you are hot, they are hot; if you are cold, they are cold.

Heating and Cooling

What's better than having a heating system and a cooling system? Having a system that doubles as a heating and cooling system at the same time. These are integral to the house and are fantastic systems. Geothermal and passive solar designs are great for all kinds of temperature regulation, both hot and cold. They should be integrated into the home when it's built. Retrofitting a house after the fact might cost you more money and trouble than it's worth.

Geothermal

We already discussed geothermal energy in a previous chapter, so we don't want to repeat too much of what was there. Geothermal is outstanding for temperature control because it draws on air that is always cooler than outside when it is hot and always warmer than when it is freezing outside.

Geothermal works by running a winding series of pipes underground, then they draw water through those pipes with a pump that will enter your home. Sometimes, these pipes will run through the floor and the walls.

The upfront costs can be high, but it is one of the most energy-efficient options for comfortably keeping the temperature out of your home.

After you dig ten feet under the ground, it's always 55 degrees Fahrenheit, no matter what time of year it is. If it's 100 degrees out, ten feet down is 55 degrees. It gets to be minus ten outside, ten feet down; it's still 55 degrees.

A geothermal heating system runs water at this temperature. It is then able to transmit it to the air using water pumps and fans. This uses some electricity but much less than a standard heating or cooling system.

Depending on the space, this can cost several thousand to build, so it will also save a lot of money if you put it together yourself. This isn't too difficult but does require a lot of work.

Geothermal is a very cool system, and there isn't any home that wouldn't benefit from a geothermal system.

Passive Solar Design

Passive solar design is clever architecture and a design of the building itself to maximize heat when you need it and minimize heat when you want it to be cooler.

There's a very important mosque in Israel called the Dome of the Rock. It is considered very important and has a very clever design. The mosque is a large stone dome. When the sun rises, it begins to heat the rock, but it takes a while for this heat to penetrate the stone and reach the inside. By the time it begins to heat the mosque, enough time has passed that the sun is already beginning its descent on the Western horizon. Then, throughout the night, the stone that was heated throughout the day cools, and by the morning, the cycle repeats itself. By simply having a dome of exactly the right amount of stone, it can keep the occupants of the mosque comfortable even in the tremendous scorching summers of the Middle East.

Passing solar design in a modern house uses techniques like this. Choosing exactly where the windows are, facing them toward the sunlight at particular times of day can have an enormous impact. Choosing where to place awnings so that the sunlight will not get in through windows, depending on where it is in the sky, also has a significant impact. The particular place you choose to keep a wood-burning stove or trees around the property in the home and how that blocks out sunlight is also a considerable factor.

Any kind of passive solar design will be wholly integrated into the house. You need to factor in things like the direction in which the wind blows. It needs to take into consideration the trees and hills nearby. A good passive solar design will be completely customized for that particular environment, so two houses with passive solar designs will often look very different depending on where they are.

For that reason, passive solar design is a little bit like feng shui. You most likely won't know how to do it, and if it's something that interests you, you are going to need to learn a heck of a lot of things before you attempt it yourself. Alternatively, you can reach out and look for architects or contractors who are familiar with passive solar design, and you can help come up with something that you are happy with.

For the sake of this book, we can't go into too much depth about solar design because that could be an entire book in itself. However, you are encouraged to look into it if you design your own home. You can get a lot of interesting ideas that cost you next to nothing but will make your heating and cooling considerably cheaper.

HEATING YOUR HOME

WOOD STOVE

The most popular way to eat in your home would be with the classic stove fireplace. These are just lovely to look at, and seeing fire gives off a cozy atmosphere. Many of these can also be used as a stovetop where pots can be placed directly on top to cook with. These things get extremely hot, so this might not be a good option if you have small children.

To operate these things, you also need to clean them regularly, and you will need to get firewood. Firewood can be found, purchased, made, and would need to be kept dry. Wood also needs to be prepared, so large logs should be split into halves, quarters, and smaller pieces.

You'll need a chimney, and if you have small children, you will absolutely need a barrier of some kind to keep your kids away. These things get HOT, and no one wants to see a toddler get a bad burn by touching one of them.

Wood stoves give really warm energy, and we don't just mean heat. They have a certain vibe that they give to a room. They come in all varieties, some very traditional and some very modern.

You'll need firewood long before actually needing wood. That means you need your wood chopped, dry, and in large supply well ahead of time before you plan on burning it. Green, freshly cut wood doesn't burn well and kicks out sparks. Put your wood someplace dry. Building a barrier over a woodpile to keep the rain off is basically mandatory. Also, you should have your logs already chopped into quarters and smaller bits. The small pieces will be needed as kindling to get the fire going, and once it's cooking, you'll want to be feeding this fire with quarter logs or at least halves. If you are chilling on a cold winter night, you don't want to have to make a trip outside to chop wood.

A major drawback of woodfire stoves is that they need to be cleaned regularly. You're going to have to get in there with a shovel and remove all of the ash. It's inside your house, so you have to be careful not to get gray dust onto everything. Ashes are a good source of compost, so be sure to add them to anything you want to use to grow.

The other drawback of the woodfire stove is, of course, fire safety. If you aren't careful about managing the fire to a good level and it gets too big, or if there's some kind of congestion in the chimney, you may find your house filling with smoke or starting a fire. Whether you have a woodfire stove or not, you should own a fire extinguisher. You are probably living far away from any fire department. Everyone needs a fire extinguisher, and that's doubly true if you are building fires inside your home.

Compost Water Heater

Compost heating sounds pretty gross, but if you do it right, you won't have to worry: It won't be gross at all. As organic material breaks down, part of the process is that as microorganisms break down the material, their life cycle releases heat. Compost heating captures this heat and moves it into a conductive source such as water, and then, you can use that water as it is almost warm, or you can pump it through a system to heat up your home.

A compost pile of wood chips can actually put out a considerable amount of heat. You'll notice it because usually, these things are left outdoors, and the heat dissipates immediately. A good compost heap gets hotter than you might think.

Running pipes through a compost heats the same way that you would for geothermal, achieving a similar effect. The heat is transferred into the pipe water. The heat is there. All you have to do is capture it. You can also use this water to heat a greenhouse if you are using one or through a radiant heat floor system. You can even find instances of people using it to heat up a hot tub all year. In the last chapter of this book, we'll go into greater detail about how to compost, but for now, it's sufficient to mention that a compost pile will get very hot, up to 150 degrees Fahrenheit. That is much hotter than most people would feel comfortable relaxing in.

Radiant Heat Floor

Try radiant floor heating if you can heat up a lot of water using composting or solar energy. Radiant floor heating looks a lot like compost heating and geothermal but in reverse. The way it works is that hot water is run in piping that zigzags underneath the floor. The pipes touch aluminum plating, which is attached to wood. Simply having the pipes making contact with the metal and wood transmits the heat, and a small amount of heat generates upward from the floor. Since heat rises, it creates a general, warm, and ambient temperature. Also, because it's just spread out, no fans are necessary. The heat doesn't just turn on and off based on what a thermometer reads.

A system like this requires a lot of piping and specially made floors. They also need a reliable pump system to keep the water moving.

People spend good money to enjoy heated flooring systems in their bathrooms. These have become very popular with those that can afford them. The radiant floor heating works on the same principle but is much cooler than the bathroom heating. They just heat one room, but you can heat your whole house. Incidentally, if you have a pet cat, they will love this.

Cooling Your Home

It's easier to warm up than it is to cool off. Keeping cool is a very tricky business that has been with humans for the entire history of our species. Our ancestors had to find solutions with much fewer resources and technology than we have now.

One of the considerations for where you choose to live will certainly involve your heat tolerance. Some people feel comfortable in warm environments, and other people just sweat, melt, and feel miserable.

You're going to be feeling pretty miserable if you move out to your new home and are deteriorating in 90-degree weather all summer long. Managing your heat is super important.

Thankfully, some options are relatively power efficient and won't require a lot of electricity.

Air Conditioning

One of the greatest modern inventions ever made is the air conditioner. We tend to think of it as a luxury good, but it has profoundly impacted human life.

Water is extremely conductive. That means electricity passes through it easily, and it collects heat easily. Imagine if you put a pot of water in the oven and set the temperature to 500 degrees Fahrenheit, letting it sit for a couple of hours. If you were to reach your hand into the oven, you would feel the heat in your hand, but it wouldn't burn you immediately. If you put your hand in the bucket, you would cook your hand. The water is very conductive, but the air isn't.

The way your body manages heat is by sweating. Since water is conductive, and saltwater is extra conductive, the heat stays in sweat as it leaves the body. The sweat falls off or dries away, carrying the heat with it. In principle, air conditioning works the same way, using a compressor and an expansion valve filled with refrigerant fluid.

You've seen your electric bills in the summer, so you already know that air conditioners are costly to keep running—these are electrically hungry machines.

That said, if the sun is shining and heating you up, they are also feeding your solar systems if you have one. This means that air conditioners are a ripe instance where you can take advantage of opportunity usage, which we covered earlier in the chapter about generating power. If you have enough solar power feeding your air conditioner, the sheets that are making you boil are the exact same energy that is going to cool you down.

Solar Chimney

Solar chimneys work on a very clever principle. You run a black pipe through the roof just like any other chimney, tape it off so that rainfall won't come in it, and put a grate in it so that animals won't climb down it. Since the pipe is black, it will absorb more solar energy and heat it up. Likewise, the air inside of the pipe will also heat up. Hot air rises. When the air in the pipe begins to rise up, it creates a suction effect that pulls air up out of the house itself.

In another portion, or portions of the house, there is also great air intake. Since the hot air at the chimney is creating a suction effect and pulling air through the house, the new air will come in through the cold vents, or the geothermal system does add cool air into the home. There's always somewhere that is relatively cool—this could be in the shade or from your geothermal system.

These systems are very different from your traditional methods. Some people have great success with these, and others don't. It's certainly something that requires thought and planning to maximize its benefits.

The major drawback of this design is that you cannot retrofit a building—it has to be designed as an integral part of the architecture.

Solar Fans

You can't go wrong with fans. Fans are cheap and don't require a lot of power. In fact, when you need to fan the most, the sun is usually shining. Solar fans are often an excellent option. Fans inside of an animal's space will help keep them cool and also help ventilate any smells. Solar fans are also recommended to be placed inside any greenhouse you build. This will help regulate the temperature inside. Plants like it hot, but they don't like it too hot.

If you're clever about it, you can find cool spaces near your house, using a fan to blow the cool air in and a different fan to push the hot air out. You can run a pipe or something through a shady area for your intake fan. You can also run an output fan at a higher level where the hottest air goes.

This is a very low-tech solution. We would not recommend using this alone. This is a good way to supplement any other cooling system that you have, but it probably won't be sufficient on its own, just like rainwater is insufficient to cover all of your water needs.

KEY CHAPTER TAKEAWAYS

- **Lesson #1: The Different Ways to Heat & Cool Your Home**

Some systems allow for both the heating and cooling of your home. Some of these are geothermal power and having a passive solar design for your home.

- **Lesson #2: Heating Systems For Your Off-Grid Home**

Some ways to heat your home off-grid are by using a wood stove, compost water heater, and radiant heat floor.

- **Lesson #3: Cooling Systems For Your Off-Grid Home**

This lesson introduces some energy-efficient ways to cool your home. These would be air conditioning, solar chimney, and solar fans.

LEARN PROVEN STRATEGIES FOR AN INDEPENDENT LIFESTYLE

You won't always have the time to devote to your venture into an off-grid life. We understand that wholeheartedly, and that's why we created this guide and even more insider lessons to make things much easier for you.

Researching, learning, and understanding all of these take a lot of time, but with us, you'll be able to cut that time to nearly half or more!

OFF-GRID TEMPERATURE SYSTEMS CHECK-IN EXERCISE

Before we proceed with the rest of the book, let's first explore where you are right now in your Off-Grid Journey.

Below, rate yourself on a scale of one to five on how accurate the statements are for you - a score of one means "not accurate," and a score of five means "very accurate."

After you have rated yourself according to the statements, add the sum total of your scores, then read "What Your Score Really Means" to determine the outcome of your results.

Check-in Statement	Rating
I know the different ways to heat and cool my off-grid home.	

I have begun researching off-grid heating systems.	
I have chosen an off-grid heating system.	
I have a set budget for my off-grid heating system.	
I have set up my heating system.	
I have begun researching off-grid cooling systems.	
I have chosen an off-grid cooling system.	
I have a set budget for my off-grid cooling system.	
I have set up my off-grid cooling system.	
I know the advantages and disadvantages of each system.	
TOTAL SCORE:	

What Your Score Really Means

Score: 0 - 15 **Warm Your Mind Up With Learning**

Comfort and living off-grid, as you probably already know, don't have to be separate things. It's also important for your health to keep the temperatures at bay. That's why it's time to review and take things seriously, for you, your family, and even your livestock, if you choose to raise any!

Score: 16 - 30

Assess Your Needs and Decide

After gathering all of your information, you need to make a final decision. Approach the subject by carefully dissecting your needs and what is most feasible for you. Lay out all the pros and cons, and soon enough, you'll find the best choice for everyone. Setting up a budget plan can also make things much clearer as well.

Score: 31+

Take Control of Your Systems

Your next big goal now is to answer: What do I need to have my ideal systems set up? Make sure to write everything down to make things infinitely easier. Take note whether the system you've chosen will need extra help in building it. Creating a realistic timeline for how things will flow can also set your expectations straight.

CHAPTER 7: OFF-GRID WASTE MANAGEMENT

In Chapter seven, you'll learn how to handle waste in your off-grid home, along with waste systems that you can choose from and a detailed description of each option.

One TEDx speaker, Lauren Singer, prefaced their presentation by proudly showing a 16-oz jar that fits all the trash they had produced over the past three years.

In their presentation, not only did they identify the causes but also provided resolutions to waste management.

According to Singer, there are three main sources of waste:

1. Food packaging

- Resolution: Try to shop in bulk

2. Product packaging

    - Resolution: Learn how to *make* all products you need

3. Organic food waste

    - Resolution: Learn how to compost

From the resolutions stated arise the benefits: things become cheaper because you learn to make things on your own. You eat better because you don't buy processed food anymore. You feel better because you're healthier. Simply put: when you eat better, feel better, and save better, you become happier.

Singer has inspired thousands of people to produce less to zero waste by being mindful of what they buy, what they make, how they manage their waste, and how to promote sustainability. The jar is proof that if they can make it possible, what's stopping you from doing the same?

"I want to be remembered for the things that I did while I was on this planet, and not for the trash that I left behind." (Singer, 2015)

Nobody really wants to deal with trash and waste. The awful stench and the bacteria are enough to make us recoil from nausea. And in the city, it's pretty much maintained for you, but once you live off-grid, this will also be one of your responsibilities to keep.

First, you'll need to think about your trash. Where will you discard that waste? There are laws in place on how to keep things sanitary, so you'll need to keep that in mind as well.

Second, you need to take into account your water waste as well; this is the water you use after bathing, washing your hands, or cleaning pretty much anything. This is called *gray*

water, and you'll need to decide on a good way to deal with it.

For you to live off-grid, you need to keep things as sanitary as possible to stay healthy and keep your home safe. Furthermore, your waste in the bathroom also needs to be managed. You need to learn about systems to put in place, and throughout this chapter, you'll discover the best one for you.

Waste management is vital and also one of the things we think about least when considering living off the grid. When you live on a plumbing and sewage system and have regular garbage collection, you don't have to think about this much. However, when waste disposal becomes your job to take care of, you will understand how important it really is.

DO NOT dump your septic waste on your property. It is gross, illegal, and dangerous. Even if animals use the wilderness as their restroom, you should not be doing the same.

Trash and Composting

Any leftover materials that you throw out, such as dinner scraps, leftover food that has gone bad, or little bits of meat on the bones of ribs you cooked the night before, can be used to fuel your garden.

There's no need to waste perfectly good materials. Even things like coffee grounds, eggshells, and ash can be great in a garden. You will definitely want to have a separate place to dispose of compostable materials and set that aside. If you own pigs, they are always happy to eat any scraps or leftovers that you are done with.

If you're doing any gardening, and you probably are, you will definitely want a compost pile.

There are two kinds of composting: hot and cold. Cold is as simple as taking the waste and putting it in a container or pile and letting them decompose.

Hot composting requires more work, but it speeds up the process. When the weather is warm, you can speed it up so that it is done in a month or two. To get faster composting, you will need oxygen, water, carbon, and nitrogen. All these things will help feed the microorganisms that will consume the matter, speeding up the rate of decay.

You can also speed this up by purchasing worms. Specifically, you need red worms, also sometimes called red wigglers. These are not hard to find. You won't use the nightcrawlers you buy for fishing or any other worm. Any place with a decent gardening supply section should be able to help you out.

Whatever bio trash you are using, you are also going to want to add nitrogen-rich material. This would include grass trimmings, leaves, tree branches, newspaper, hay, cardboard, and wood chips. Any of these materials should be mixed in with your composting material.

If you aren't getting much rain, you'll need to water the pile regularly, just like it's a garden of trash. You're not trying to get totally soaked—you just want to add enough water so that the microorganisms can do their job. However, don't add so much that you drown your red wigglers. If you can put your hand inside of it and feel it's producing a lot of heat, you are doing it right.

About every week or so, you should turn your pile over and let it mix. To do this with the shovel or pitchfork, just keep it moving. Make sure it's getting oxygen in the center. At this point, it should be getting very hot, up to 150 degrees.

Your compost is done when it stops putting out lots of heat. It should start looking like dirt again. At that point, it is perfect for your garden, so go ahead and transplant that dirt and all your red wigglers into their new home.

TRASH

Anything that isn't compostable, biodegradable, or burnable, such as plastic, should be placed in a container and set aside. Since you don't have a trash removal service coming to your location, you will need to take it to a dump yourself or arrange for someone to come and get it. Hopefully, the amount of this kind of waste will diminish over time, and these trips will become less frequent.

BURN

Some things are perfectly fine to burn, such as wood, cotton, cloth, paper towel rolls, and dryer lint. Again, don't set anything on fire that will create toxicity. Don't try burning plastic or metal with paint on it or something else you wouldn't want to breathe.

When burning things, always do so responsibly. Don't start a fire if you live in a dry climate during a dry spell. Starting fires can be very risky in certain places like Wyoming and Colorado. If you are going to use a burn barrel, just be careful, and be sure to have a fire extinguisher close by.

We're sure we sound like a broken record, but here it is: Make sure it is legal to burn your trash. Different places have different rules. If you're deep enough back from the road, probably no one will see you, but it needs to be said.

GRAY WATER

Gray water is dirty water from your sink or shower—this isn't toilet water. It's simple enough to get rid of so long as you aren't using soaps and detergents with harmful chemicals. If you are using all-natural stuff to wash your body and your dishes, then this water can simply be grounded out of the house and dropped onto the soil working to be reabsorbed by the earth. Be sure that nothing you deposit is going to be harmful and harm the plants or wildlife out there or be something that you don't want anything to do with the groundwater.

Make sure nothing that goes into the gray water is harmful. You can check all your labels and investigate if you have any doubts. If you are using harmful detergents and soaps, you can always put those into a septic system.

Depending on how you set up your water system, there are many ways to capture and separate your gray water from your septic system. It can be simply diverted into a bucket. As simple as that sounds, that's completely viable. Gray water could also be diverted toward a particular use that you have in mind. For example, gray water, provided that it is clean enough that it won't hurt plants, could potentially be diverted into the yard to be reabsorbed by the soil. If you are especially confident of the quality of your gray water, you could even divert it to your garden to water plants.

Gray water that is dirty can also be used to flush toilets, wash your clothes, or wash your car. That is a good way to get multiple uses out of one batch of water and get much more efficient use for it. That's definitely preferable to dumping it in a septic system.

Septic System

Probably the most popular option is to install a septic system. A septic system is a gigantic tank buried underground just like a water tank, but instead of holding water, it holds everything you flush down the toilet. If you have any kind of internal plumbing in your home, you are definitely going to need this. We don't want the septic system boiling, and we don't want it freezing. Both will be a worse disaster than bursting the water tanks.

Tanks have a hatch, and you will need to periodically have a waste removal truck come and suck out the waste that is stored there. Depending on the size of your tank and how many people live in your home, this could be only once every few years.

Outhouse

It may not be surprising to know that most people don't want to use an outhouse. Outhouses are a very old way of doing things. They don't require any water and are very easy to build. To use the bathroom, you'll have to leave your house, and if it's in the dead of winter, that's not too much fun.

If you don't want to live a life with an outhouse, they might be useful as a start-up way to have a restroom until you are completely building a more permanent one. If your properties are particularly large, you might find that putting in an outhouse at the far end will be helpful when walking around so that you don't have to hike all the way back to your home for number two.

Composting Toilet

This isn't very attractive for everyone, but it's actually really great. A composting toilet does not use water. If you remember from the earlier chapter on setting up your water, toilet flushes account for a huge amount of the water that you go through.

Composting toilets can be purchased or built from scratch. You won't need a septic system so long as you have a suitable means of disposing of your gray water.

Essentially, this is a system to dump in a bucket and turn your own waste into human compost. Yes, that sounds pretty gross, but it's not as bad as you think. You save a lot of water, and it's very eco-friendly.

Your waste is caught in a bucket with sawdust. The sawdust works a lot like cat litter; it absorbs your waste and also cuts down on the smell. The drier, the better. Some have two separate chambers: one for urine and one for feces.

In your home, you're going to want a fan system to ventilate odors out of your home. Some water mixed with vinegar in a spray bottle can also help a lot.

When you've got a full bucket, haul it out to your composting heap. This is by far the greenest option of all of them. If you are particularly concerned about conservation, this is your best bet.

One way to know who your real friends are is to invite them for a soak in a hot tub hooked up to a compost heat system, heated using your own human manure.

KEY CHAPTER TAKEAWAYS

- **Lesson #1: Composting & Dealing With Trash Off-Grid**

Disposing of your trash will depend solely on you. You must learn how to compost and properly throw out the correct trash.

- **Lesson #2: Disposing of Gray Water**

Gray water is used water from your sink or shower. Some people also reuse it for other purposes if the water isn't harmful. You will need to choose a way to collect and dispose of it.

- **Lesson #3: The Different Systems For Waste Management**

The different types of waste systems are septic systems, outhouse, and composting toilets. The prices of each vary, and some will require a professional team to handle them.

THE BREAKTHROUGH YOU'RE WAITING FOR

Many times, we're really just waiting for that big break for ourselves, aren't we? We're waiting to win that lottery ticket, get that promotion, or even just for normal life to come again.

But the thing is, waiting without action won't do anything to change our lives. So today, we're urging you to take hold of your life once again. Your breakthrough is near and possible if you do something about it.

We created this guide to help you jumpstart your journey, but if you want to take it even further, we're here to help.

OFF-GRID WASTE MANAGEMENT CHECK-IN EXERCISE

Before we proceed with the rest of the book, let's first explore where you are right now in your Off-Grid Journey.

Below, rate yourself on a scale of one to five on how accurate the statements are for you - a score of one means "not accurate," and a score of five means "very accurate."

After you have rated yourself according to the statements, add the sum total of your scores, then read "What Your Score Really Means" to determine the outcome of your results.

Check-in Statement	Rating
I no longer depend on waste systems in the city.	
I know how to compost.	
I know how to dispose of gray water.	
I know the different kinds of off-grid waste management systems.	
I have researched the different options for waste management.	
I have chosen a waste management system for my off-grid home.	
I know the advantages and disadvantages of waste systems.	
I have a set budget for my chosen waste management system.	
I know how to dispose of trash in my off-grid home.	
TOTAL SCORE:	

What Your Score Really Means

Score: 0 - 15

Declutter Your Mind

Right now, you must be seeing how there's so much needed to fix to live off-grid. And you're right; it's no piece of cake. There are a lot of responsibilities that go into it, even your waste management!

And so, supplying yourself with enough knowledge is essential, but taking a breather, stepping back, and looking at the bigger picture can help you even more. Clear your head and set your goal in place.

Score: 16 - 30

Organize Your Options

You are doing a great job in taking in enough knowledge on the subject, but you still need to take a few steps ahead. Now that you know more, it's time to organize the variety of options set before you. List down all the pros and cons, your set budget, and

those you like the most in general. Carefully considering all the factors will help you make a final decision.

Score: 31+

Take Action

Once you've chosen your ideal wastage system and you know exactly how it'll function in your home, you are now ready to set things up yourself. If you can take it on your own, purchase all the materials, resources, and items you need to begin. If you need extra

help to get things done, research and contact the right people for the job. Keep reviewing how things will be set up and create another timeline for this process. You will now be well on your way to completing your off-grid journey and finally enjoying it for yourself.

An Outline to Start Your New Home

This is the order of operations to get your homestead off the ground. You can use this as a general outline or a worksheet, a place to get your mind moving and to get the process of planning moving.

Step One: Make a Decision

This is the biggest step of all. Simply choose if you want to do it. You will need to consider if this is good for your family overall. Make sure that everyone involved understands and is happy to participate. If you have a spouse and children, they need to be okay with all this stuff, too.

Step Two: Planning

The more planning you do, the easier and smoother all the rest of the steps are.

- Figure out your budget.
- Research locations.
- Choose a state and county.
- If you are moving far away, you will have to figure out work if you can't do it remotely—that might mean looking for a new job.
- Calculate your power consumption; estimate how much power you can generate.

- Calculate your water consumption; estimate how much water you can produce.

You want to have an estimate of all the material costs. There's the price of land, and if you live in a state with property taxes, you'll have to add that to your calculations as well. If there's going to be an interruption to your income, that's going to have to be figured out.

You also want a buffer. It is a sure thing that things will go wrong. That's not an off-grid thing; that's a life thing. You might make an error, wire your electrical system incorrectly, and accidentally torch your inverter. You might have horrendous weather that slows you down. Maybe a clever fox finds their way into your chicken coop. Things always go wrong, and they take time, energy, and money to make them right.

Step Three: Find Land

Once all the other considerations have been weighed and you know what you are looking for, go find it and buy it. The two most important things are:

- A place where you are actually allowed to live off-grid without too much interference from red tape and regulation.
- A source of water.

If you are going to need a deep well, get that scheduled and have them come to do that early. This spot is a bust if they can't find water and there is no other good source. There's no reason to sink more money or energy into it. Provided that goes well (no pun intended), carry on! If you don't have a mailbox, you will want to get a P.O. box to receive mail and packages.

Step Four: Make a Shelter

Move to your new place. You're going to need a place to sleep. It's fine to start with something small like a camper, a trailer, or even a van if you can stand it. It's definitely recommended that you start in the spring when the temperature is just starting to warm up, and you have more warm months to get started.

If you have a family, they don't all have to come at this point. They can hang back while you get things prepared. It might require some trips back and forth; it might be a process.

Step Four can stay with the temporary place, or you can build a more permanent system as you go along. Step Four also fits into every other step.

Step Five: Get Your Baseline

You have a temporary shelter. You also need electricity, water, and food.

Get yourself a gas-powered generator. This is a temporary power source just until you can get your sustainable system operational.

You need water. You can have it delivered, or you can haul it yourself.

Food will be the same grocery-bought stuff you always use.

You'll also need a place to relieve yourself. If you have a trailer or a camper, that's covered. If not, you will need a bucket full of sawdust or an outhouse for the time being.

Garbage can be put in a can or bags and taken to the dump as needed.

Depending on how far out your new home is, you may not be able to get a signal. You need to get some kind of communication system up as quickly as possible. You can buy a signal booster and attach it to a small tower. That can give you a lot more range. If that doesn't do the trick, consider getting a satellite Internet service.

You're going to want to be able to call for help in an emergency, check the weather, and look up how-to guides when you run into things you don't know how to do. Communication is mandatory.

You now have your baseline. You have all the basic needs covered. As this project continues, each one of those will be replaced with a sustainable system.

STEP SIX: ELECTRICITY

Set up your electrical system. You need your solar panels and/or wind turbines up. You need to get them hooked up safely.

You need a location to house the power system. That probably means building a shed to house everything away from the elements, especially water.

Run your connections from your power source. Hook up your AC inverter, batteries, charge controller, fuses, bus bars, etc. Get that all wired up. Contact an electrician if you need to. Safety first!

STEP SEVEN: WATER

Now that you have power, you can operate pumps. Once you can have operational pumps, you can get water. Your next task is to hook up to your water source. You are in business if you have tanks/cisterns, pipes, and filters ready to go. If you have a house built, that means hooking that up.

Life just got a lot easier. Also, you can now heat your water, which is a big deal if you've been living without it for a little while.

Step Eight: Waste

Now that you have water, you can hook that up to a septic system. Congratulations if you were using a bucket before because you can now use a toilet!

Step Nine: Start Your Farm

Now that you have working water, you can start your farm and your composting.

Set up a garden and/or build a greenhouse, and get started on any planting.

If you are keeping animals, build them a coop, barn, fenced-in area, or whatever they need. You are really rolling now!

Step Ten: Do Whatever You Want

You should have all the basic ingredients for self-sustenance: shelter, electricity, water, and food. You can use the toilet and take a shower.

These may not be completely up and running quite yet—you may have hiccups. If necessary, there's no shame in supplementing yourself with visits to the store if you need to.

Where you go from here is entirely up to you. You may find that you want to start upgrading some new systems. You may find that one of the systems you've already built can be built better or optimized.

All the necessities are taken care of. What you do next is whatever you want to do!

CONCLUSION

Now that we're at the end of the book, you may have started working out a rough sketch of the home you want to build. Maybe you've got your ideal state narrowed down to a few. You've got some ideas about what your home will look like, how you think you can power it, and how to supply water to it.

That's good—get that rough sketch, but don't try to put the ink down on this paper in your mind just yet. Once you get started, there are going to be a lot of changes and adaptations that you will make along the way. Don't get too hung up on a perfect and idealized version of your homestead. Instead, you and the land should meet each other halfway and figure it out together.

This book will not be nearly enough to teach you everything you should or want to know.

There is a lot more to raising chickens and growing tomatoes than we could possibly cover in these few pages. One of the most important things you should do is continue learning.

When you decide you want to set up your own AC converter but don't know the first thing about electricity, you will have to read another book about that. Just absorb as much as you can. There are so many other homesteaders and off-grid people out there. There are many forums full of people that are eager to talk to you and share tips. There are countless websites full of great information that can teach you a lot and point you in the right direction.

We know that you're curious about moving off-grid, but at this stage, you're probably more than curious. If you didn't like the idea or it didn't sound like it was for you, you probably would have stopped reading this book halfway through earlier, but because you read it from the front to the back, you're still interested.

If you are so interested and have the means and opportunity, We would definitely recommend that you take this on. This is not something we would encourage a half-interested person to do, but if you have made it to the conclusion of this book, you are feeling excited, and you are thinking about all the different projects that you could do and the only things you want to learn, then we say follow that instinct. Take it to its ultimate conclusion.

Find your own independence, self-reliance, and environmental consideration, and build yourself a place where you will be happy and free.

One Last Thing

We spend so much of our modern lives making things that only exist virtually. Many of us spend a third of our day operating computers. Money people collate tables and leverage financial instruments to make money. Software engineers write complex algebraic formulas to develop a cell phone app. Marketing people look at charts and figures that tell them what people want without ever talking to people.

So much of what we do isn't material. It exists as an abstraction. People are aching to do something real, tangible, and right here. You'll see it in little ways.

You see people taking on knitting as a hobby, which was formerly considered something that old women do, but young women have suddenly taken an interest in crocheting and other crafts—things that require physical contact.

People are suddenly taking up hobbies like ax throwing and bowhunting.

People get on the Internet and look at videos of people building furniture from scratch.

People start brewing their own beer at home.

People seem to be yearning for another era where people worked with their hands, and when they were done working, there was something tangible in front of them—something that they could be proud of. Instead of working a job and seeing numbers appear in a bank account so they can purchase objects made on the other side of the world, they just want to make something themselves and have it. They want to see the fruits of their own labor and hold on to it like a trophy or a memento—some kind of physical reminder that they can be proud of.

You can feel it too, can't you? Building a life off-grid is not weird. What's weird is living in tiny concrete boxes, stacked hundreds of feet tall, in a gray, concrete place where you see thousands of people walk past you every day, and you don't know a single one of them.

If you want to try something new—if you want to craft the environment into a place just for you—then you are like many others. Many of them are less smart and talented than you are. If they can do it, you can, too.

References

Average Annual Precipitation for Missouri. (n.d.). Current Results. https://www.currentresults.com/Weather/Missouri/average-yearly-precipitation.php

Buri, R. (2017). Solar-roof-solar-energy. In *pixabay.com.* https://cdn.pixabay.com/photo/2017/08/21/20/29/solar-2666770_960_720.jpg

Cloud, B. (2018). Lake in forest. In *unsplash.com.* https://images.unsplash.com/photo-1542849922-a7e0aeb0ff84?ixlib=rb-1.2.1&ixid=MnwxMjA3fDB8MHxwaG90by1wYWdlfHx8fGVufDB8fHx8&auto=format&fit=crop&w=1534&q=80

Dais, W. (2011). chicken-coop-farm-chickens-coop. In *pixabay.com.* https://cdn.pixabay.com/photo/2014/05/14/08/02/chicken-coop-343942_960_720.jpg

Ellis, K. (2018). Triangle house. In *unsplash.com.* https://images.unsplash.com/photo-1525113990976-399835c43838?ixid=MnwxMjA3fDB8MHxwaG90by1wYWdlfHx8fGVufDB8fHx8&ixlib=rb-1.2.1&auto=format&fit=crop&w=700&q=80

Giannatti, D. (2019). Outhouse door. In *unsplash.com.* https://images.unsplash.com/photo-1548097751-193b78ef6823?ixid=MnwxMjA3fDB8MHxwaG90by1wYWdlfHx8fGVufDB8fHx8&ixlib=rb-1.2.1&auto=format&fit=crop&w=639&q=80

Glenn, K. (2018). Green dome near brown wooden dock. In *unsplash.com.* https://images.unsplash.com/photo-1521401830884-6c03c1c87ebb?ixlib=rb-

1.2.1&ixid=MnwxMjA3fDB8MHxwaG90by1wYWdlfHx8fGVufDB8fHx8&auto=format&fit=crop&w=1500&q=80

Gomez, J. (2019). Wood stove. In *unsplash.com.* https://images.unsplash.com/photo-1564848534637-f57f9b1eb36e?ixlib=rb-1.2.1&ixid=MnwxMjA3fDB8MHxwaG90by1wYWdlfHx8fGVufDB8fHx8&auto=format&fit=crop&w=632&q=80

Gruebner, O., Rapp, M. A., Adli, M., Kluge, U., Galea, S., & Heinz, A. (2017). Cities and Mental Health. *Deutsches Arzteblatt international*, *114*(8), 121–127. https://doi.org/10.3238/arztebl.2017.0121

How We Use Water. (n.d.). United States Environmental Protection Agency (EPA). https://www.epa.gov/watersense/how-we-use-water

Jesus, J. (n.d.). Photo-of-man-standing-surrounded-by-green-leaf-plants. In *pexels.com.* https://images.pexels.com/photos/1084540/pexels-photo-1084540.jpeg?auto=compress&cs=tinysrgb&dpr=2&h=650&w=940

Lechner, G. (2020). Black and white wooden house. In *unsplash.com.* https://images.unsplash.com/photo-1580856942656-d4416b6e5c2e?ixlib=rb-1.2.1&ixid=MnwxMjA3fDB8MHxwaG90by1wYWdlfHx8fGVufDB8fHx8&auto=format&fit=crop&w=1563&q=80

Living, O. G. (2020, February 26). *How to go off grid for $10k or less.* Off Grid Living. https://offgridliving.net/go-off-grid-10k/

PublicDomainPictures. (2010). Clean-countryside-drink-garden. In *pixabay.com.* https://cdn.pixabay.com/photo/2012/03/03/22/59/clean-21479_960_720.jpg

Timmer, K. (2019). Brown wood house. In *unsplash.com.* https://images.unsplash.com/photo-1568659585069-

facb248c4935?ixlib=rb-1.2.1&ixid=MnwxMjA3fDB8MHxwaG90by1wYWdlfHx8fGVufDB8fHx8&auto=format&fit=crop&w=1500&q=80

www.ingramcontent.com/pod-product-compliance
Lightning Source LLC
LaVergne TN
LVHW010945100826
845153LV00002B/147